Hollington on Shareholders' Rights

HOLLINGTON ON SHAREHOLDERS' RIGHTS

FIRST SUPPLEMENT TO THE EIGHTH EDITION

ROBIN HOLLINGTON, QC, M.A. (OXON), LL.M. (PENN.)
Bencher of Lincoln's Inn

SWEET & MAXWELL

First Edition 1990
Second Edition 1994
Third Edition 1999
Fourth Edition 2004
Fifth Edition 2007
Sixth Edition 2010
Seventh Edition 2013
Eighth Edition 2017

Published in 2018 by Thomson Reuters, trading as Sweet & Maxwell.
Thomson Reuters is registered in England & Wales, Company No.1679046.
Registered Office and address for service:
5 Canada Square, Canary Wharf, London, E14 5AQ.
For further information on our products and services, visit
http://www.sweetandmaxwell.co.uk.

Computerset by Sweet & Maxwell.
Printed and bound by CPI Group (UK) Ltd, Croydon, CR0 4YY.

No natural forests were destroyed to make this product: only farmed timber was used and replanted.

A CIP catalogue record for this book is available from the British Library.

ISBN: 978-0-414-07022-6

Crown copyright material is reproduced with the permission of the Controller of HMSO and the Queen's Printer for Scotland.

All rights reserved. No part of this publication may be reproduced, or transmitted in any form, or by any means, or stored in any retrieval system of any nature, without prior written permission, except for permitted fair dealing under the Copyright, Designs and Patents Act 1988, or in accordance with the terms of a licence issued by the Copyright Licensing Agency in respect of photocopying and/or reprographic reproduction. Application for permission for other use of copyright material, including permission to reproduce extracts in other published works, should be made to the publishers. Full acknowledgement of the author, publisher and source must be given.

© 2018 Robin Hollington

Preface to the Supplement to the Eighth Edition

Harris v Microfusion 2003-2 LLP [2017] 1 B.C.L.C. 305 (CA), noted in this Supplement under para.6-20, has laid to rest, short of the Supreme Court, one of the classic controversies as to the scope of the "fraud on minority" exception to the rule in Foss v Harbottle. Under the new statutory derivative claim regime, there is no requirement that the defendant directors should have benefited personally from their alleged wrongdoing: so, for example, if the directors acted negligently causing loss to the company, then a statutory derivative claim would in principle lie. The Court of Appeal held in the *Harris* case that, if the derivative claim is to be brought under the common law regime, then, absent fraud, it must be shown that the directors benefited from their wrongdoing. The Court of Appeal did not explain why as a matter of principle this should be the law, when Parliament has so clearly thought otherwise when enacting the statutory regime.

As noted under para.11-20 in this Supplement, recent cases show how narrow is the so-called "exception", established by *Giles v Rhind*, to the rule against the recovery of reflective loss, i.e. a shareholder cannot sue for the company's loss. The exception only applies where the defendant's wrongdoing has made it legally impossible for the company to sue: *Garcia v Marex Financial Ltd* [2018] EWCA Civ 1468, approving *Peak Hotels and Resorts Ltd v Tarek Investments Ltd* [2015] EWHC 3048 (Ch), and *St Vincent European General Partner Ltd v Robinson* [2018] EWHC 1230 (Comm).

The starting point in determining whether the conduct of the majority is unfair for the purposes of the unfair prejudice remedy is whether the majority have acted in breach of the "bargain" between the shareholders: see Principle 14. It is clearly established that this "bargain" is not confined to legally enforceable contracts. But what sort of agreements or understandings, short of legally enforceable contracts, suffice for this purpose? In the leading case of *O'Neill v Phillips*, Lord Hoffmann held that the court should for this purpose stick to settled principles of equity as opposed to a test of "legitimate expectation" or some indefinite notion of fairness. He was explicit as to why he favoured a narrower, clearer, test of unfairness, namely that of enabling lawyers to advise their clients as to the likely outcome of a dispute. But that apparently neat solution gives rise to the obvious questions: (i) given that the statutory unfair prejudice remedy uses the broad language of "fairness", why should the courts think that Parliament intended them to stick to settled principles of equity? (ii) do principles of equity in fact provide clear and correct guidance in this context? See the doubts expressed about this aspect of Lord Hoffmann's judgment in para.7-36. These issues have given rise to confusingly different treatments in three recent cases, two of which were concerned with the statutory unfair prejudice remedy and one of which concerned equitable remedies. In the first category are *VB Football Assets v Blackpool Football Club (Properties) Ltd* [2017] EWHC 2767 (Ch), noted in this Supplement under para.7-94, and *Re Edwardian Group Ltd* [2018] EWHC 1715 (Ch), noted in this Supplement under para.7-99. In the second category is *Generator Developments Ltd v Lidl UK GmbH* [2018] EWCA Civ 396, noted in this Supplement under para.11-60. So it is open to question whether he succeeded in enabling lawyers to advise their clients as to the likely outcome of any dispute.

A very important, and often the most important in practice, issue in the application of the unfair prejudice remedy is the valuation of the shares of the aggrieved minority. The majority will often be prepared to buy out the minority, the obvious solution to most disputes between shareholders where there has been an irretrievable breakdown in relations, but at what price? Minority stakes in unlisted companies seldom have any significant market value, simply because there is unlikely to be any market for the shares in question. However, why should the wrongdoing majority be allowed to acquire the minority's shares at such a market value and thus in a sense be rewarded for its own wrongdoing? Since the courts have invariably started the valuation process by valuing the issued share capital as a whole, this conundrum is usually analysed in terms of whether a "discount" should be applied to reflect the minority status of the stake of the aggrieved minority and if so how much that "discount" should be. These issues are discussed in paras. 8-149 to 8-158 of the main work. They were revisited in the recent case of *Re Edwardian Group Ltd* [2018] EWHC 1715 (Ch), noted under para.8-158 in this Supplement, where the court came up with the Solomonic but not entirely persuasive solution of splitting the difference between the market value and the "marriage value", i.e. the additional value created by adding the minority to the majority shareholding. A completely different and more arbitrary approach was adopted in *Re CF Booth Ltd* [2017] EWHC 457 (Ch), also noted under para.8-158 in this Supplement.

It is a wholly unsatisfactory state of the law that lawyers cannot give clear and confident advice as to the value of a minority stake.

This valuation issue, together with the above-mentioned issue as to what constitutes unfairness, raise a fundamental question as to the purpose of the unfair prejudice remedy: Lord Hoffmann sought to address this fundamental question in *O'Neill v Phillips*, but it is considered that the time is ripe for judicial reconsideration or legislative intervention.

Given the difficulty that lawyers often have in advising their clients as to the likely outcome in a shareholders' dispute, it is not surprising that the courts, perhaps losing faith in the litigation process which is their raison d'etre, are keen to help the parties to compromise their differences as soon as possible without incurring huge expense. Under para.9-32 of this Supplement, reference is made to the noble attempt by the courts of Victoria, Australia, to persuade the parties to go down the path of compromise. Perhaps UK courts could do more in this regard. But one has to recognise that there are some disputes which are peculiarly resistant to compromise: for example, where emotions run high because of a perceived breach of trust, or where a party is well off and can afford to litigate at enormous expense.

Robin Hollington QC
Lincoln's Inn
London
19 September 2018

How to use this supplement

This is the First Supplement to the Eighth Edition of *Hollington on Shareholders' Rights* and has been compiled according to the structure of the main volume.

At the beginning of each chapter of this Supplement, a mini table of contents of the sections in the main volume has been included. Where a heading in this table of contents has been marked by the symbol ■ there is relevant information in this Supplement to which you should refer.

Within each chapter, updating information is referenced to the relevant paragraph in the main volume.

TABLE OF CONTENTS

Preface to the Supplement to the Eighth Edition	v
How to use this supplement	vii
Table of Cases	xi
Table of Statutes	xix
Table of Statutory Instruments	xxi

CHAPTER 2
BROAD PRINCIPLES 1

CHAPTER 3
THE BARGAIN BETWEEN SHAREHOLDERS 3

CHAPTER 4
DIRECTORS' DUTIES 7

CHAPTER 5
MAJORITY RULE AND EQUITABLE CONSTRAINTS 15

CHAPTER 6
THE DERIVATIVE CLAIM 19

CHAPTER 7
THE UNFAIR PREJUDICE REMEDY: PRINCIPLES 23

CHAPTER 8
UNFAIR PREJUDICE 2: REMEDIES 39

CHAPTER 9
UNFAIR PREJUDICE 3: PRACTICE AND PROCEDURE 49

CHAPTER 10
WINDING-UP ON THE JUST AND EQUITABLE GROUND 55

CHAPTER 11
PERSONAL RIGHTS OF SHAREHOLDERS 57

CHAPTER 12
FOREIGN ELEMENT 65

CHAPTER 14
LIMITED AND LIMITED LIABILITY PARTNERSHIPS 67

Index

TABLE OF CASES

Aas v Benham [1891] 2 Ch. 244 CA 4-68
Aberdeen Rly Co v Blaikie Bros (1854) 1 Macq 461; [1843-60] All E.R. Rep. 249 4-71
Abouraya v Sigmund [2014] EWHC 277 (Ch); [2015] B.C.C. 503 6-20
Alcatel Australia Ltd v Scarcella (1998) 44 NSWLR 349 3-26
Allied Business & Financial Consultants Ltd, Re; sub nom. O'Donnell v Shanahan [2009]
   EWCA Civ 751; [2009] B.C.C. 822; [2009] 2 B.C.L.C. 666........................... 4-68
AMT Coffee Ltd, Re; sub nom. McCallum-Toppin v McCallum-Toppin [2018] EWHC
   1562 (Ch) 9-08
Annacott Holdings Ltd, Re; sub nom. Tobian Properties Ltd, Re; Attwood v Maidment;
   Maidment v Attwood [2012] EWCA Civ 998; [2013] Bus. L.R. 753; [2013] B.C.C. 98;
   [2013] 2 B.C.L.C. 567 9-47
Annaott Holdings Ltd, Re; sub nom. Maidment v Attwood; Tobian Properties Ltd, Re;
   Attwood v Maidment [2012] EWHC 1662 (Ch) 8-131
Apex Global Management Ltd v Fi Call Ltd [2013] EWHC 1652 (Ch); [2014] B.C.C. 286 ... 8-37
Arnold v Britton [2015] UKSC 36; [2015] A.C. 1619; [2015] 2 W.L.R. 1593; [2016] 1 All
   E.R. 1; [2015] H.L.R. 31; [2015] 2 P. & C.R. 14; [2015] L. & T.R. 25; [2015] C.I.L.L.
   3689.. 3-19
Arrow Nominees Inc v Blackledge [2000] C.P. Rep. 59; [2001] B.C.C. 591; [2000] 2
   B.C.L.C. 167... 7-204
ASA Resource Group Plc, Re; sub nom. Ning v Dearing [2018] EWHC 1102 (Ch) 8-14, 9-17
Astor Management AG v Atalaya Mining Plc [2017] EWHC 425 (Comm); [2018] 1 All
   E.R. (Comm) 547; [2017] Bus. L.R. 1634; [2017] 1 Lloyd's Rep. 476; [2017] 2
   B.C.L.C. 119; [2017] 1 C.L.C. 72... 3-26
Attorney General of Belize v Belize Telecom Ltd [2009] UKPC 10; [2009] 1 W.L.R.
   1988; [2009] 2 All E.R. 1127; [2009] 2 All E.R. (Comm) 1; [2009] Bus. L.R. 1316;
   [2009] B.C.C. 433; [2009] 2 B.C.L.C. 148.. 3-19
Aurora Funds Management Ltd v Torchlight GP Ltd unreported, 27 April 2018 (CICA) 10-61
Badyal v Badyal [2018] EWHC 68 (Ch) 7-117, 7-136, 10-53
Ball v Hughes; sub nom. PV Solar Solutions Ltd (In Liquidation), Re [2017] EWHC 3228
   (Ch); [2018] B.C.C. 196; [2018] 1 B.C.L.C. 58; [2018] B.P.I.R. 561................. 4-20, 7-154
Bankside Hotels Ltd, Re; Pedersen (Thameside) Ltd, Re; G&G Properties Ltd, Re; sub
   nom. Griffith v Gourgey [2018] EWHC 1035 (Ch) 8-01, 9-30
Banner Homes Holdings Ltd (formerly Banner Homes Group Plc) v Luff Developments
   Ltd [2000] Ch. 372; [2000] 2 W.L.R. 772; [2000] 2 All E.R. 117; [2000] 2 B.C.L.C.
   269; [2000] W.T.L.R. 473; (1999-2000) 2 I.T.E.L.R. 525; [2000] E.G. 15 (C.S.); (2000)
   97(6) L.S.G. 37; (2000) 97(6) L.S.G. 35; (2000) 144 S.J.L.B. 83; (2000) 79 P. & C.R.
   D29 11-58
Barclay Pharmaceuticals Ltd v Waypharm LP [2013] EWHC 503 (Comm); [2014] 2 All
   E.R. (Comm) 82; [2013] 2 B.C.L.C. 551 11-18
Barclays Bank Plc v Landgraf [2014] EWHC 503 (Comm); [2015] 1 All E.R. (Comm)
   720... 3-19
Baturina v Chistyakov [2017] EWHC 1049 (Comm) 11-58
Beppler & Jacobson Ltd, Re; sub nom. Leibson Corp v Toc Investments Corp [2018]
   EWCA Civ 763; [2018] 2 Costs L.R. 293...................................... 3-18, 8-123
Bhullar v Bhullar; sub nom. Bhullar Bros Ltd, Re [2003] EWCA Civ 424; [2003] B.C.C.
   711; [2003] 2 B.C.L.C. 241; [2003] W.T.L.R. 1397; (2003) 147 S.J.L.B. 421; [2003]
   N.P.C. 45... 4-71
Blackmore v Richardson. *See* Richardson v Blackmore 7-202
Blindley Heath Investments Ltd v Bass; sub nom. Dixon v Blindley Heath Investments
   Ltd [2015] EWCA Civ 1023; [2017] Ch. 389; [2017] 3 W.L.R. 166; [2016] 4 All E.R.
   490; [2017] 1 All E.R. (Comm) 319... 8-131
Blue Index Ltd, Re; sub nom. Murrell v Swallow [2014] EWHC 2680 (Ch) 8-134, 8-158
Boardman v Phipps; sub nom. Phipps v Boardman [1967] 2 A.C. 46; [1966] 3 W.L.R.
   1009; [1966] 3 All E.R. 721; (1966) 110 S.J. 853 4-71
Bray v Ford [1896] A.C. 44 HL 4-71
Bristol & West Building Society v Mothew (t/a Stapley & Co); sub nom. Mothew v
   Bristol & West Building Society [1998] Ch. 1; [1997] 2 W.L.R. 436; [1996] 4 All E.R.

698; [1997] P.N.L.R. 11; (1998) 75 P. & C.R. 241; [1996] E.G. 136 (C.S.); (1996) 146
    N.L.J. 1273; (1996) 140 S.J.L.B. 206; [1996] N.P.C. 126 CA (Civ Div) 11-46
British Midland Tool Ltd v Midland International Tooling Ltd [2003] EWHC 466 (Ch);
    [2003] 2 B.C.L.C. 523 4-71
Brunninghausen v Glavanics (1999) 46 N.S.W.L.R. 538 11-46
Brunninghausen v Glavanics [1999] NSWCA 199; (1999) 32 A.C.S.R. 294 11-46
BTI 2014 LLC v Sequana SA; BAT Industries Plc v Sequana SA [2018] 1 B.C.L.C. 623;
    [2016] EWHC 1686 (Ch); [2017] Bus. L.R. 82; [2017] 1 B.C.L.C. 453 4-20
Burberry Group Plc v Fox-Davies; sub nom. Fox-Davies v Burberry Plc [2017] EWCA
    Civ 1129; [2018] Bus. L.R. 332; [2017] B.C.C. 387 5-23
Burger King Corpn v Hungry Jack's Pty Ltd [2001] NSWCA 187; 69 NSWLR 558 3-26
Burnden Holdings (UK) Ltd v Fielding [2018] UKSC 14; [2018] 2 W.L.R. 885; [2018] 2
    All E.R. 1083 4-133
Caparo Industries Plc v Dickman [1990] 2 A.C. 605; [1990] 2 W.L.R. 358; [1990] 1 All
    E.R. 568; [1990] B.C.C. 164; [1990] B.C.L.C. 273; [1990] E.C.C. 313; [1955-95]
    P.N.L.R. 523; (1990) 87(12) L.S.G. 42; (1990) 140 N.L.J. 248; (1990) 134 S.J. 494 HL 11-12
Certain Ltd Partners in Henderson PFI Secondary Fund II LLP v Henderson PFI
    Secondary Fund II LP [2012] EWHC 3259 (Comm); [2013] Q.B. 934; [2013] 2 W.L.R.
    1297; [2013] 3 All E.R. 887; [2013] 2 All E.R. (Comm) 189; [2012] 2 C.L.C. 905 6-22
CF Booth Ltd, Re [2017] EWHC 457 (Ch) 7-153, 8-158, 8-164
Cha v Staray Capital Ltd unreported 13 February 13 (BVI) 7-92
Charterhouse Capital Ltd, Re; sub nom. Arbuthnott v Bonnyman [2015] EWCA Civ 536;
    [2015] B.C.C. 574; [2015] 2 B.C.L.C. 627 .... 5-46, 7-52
Cheung Hon Wah v Cheung Kam Wah [2005] HKEC 765 8-30
Children's Investment Fund Foundation (UK) v Attorney General [2017] EWHC 1379
    (Ch); [2018] Ch. 371; [2018] 2 W.L.R. 259; [2018] 2 All E.R. 504; [2018] 1 B.C.L.C.
    677. 5-31
Choudhary v Bhattar; sub nom. Choudhury v Bhatter [2009] EWCA Civ 1176; [2010] 2
    All E.R. 1031; [2010] 2 All E.R. (Comm) 419; [2010] 2 B.C.L.C. 17; [2010] I.L.Pr. 8;
    (2009) 159 N.L.J. 1628. 12-27
Cia de Seguros Imperio v Heath (REBX) Ltd (formerly CE Heath & Co (America) Ltd);
    sub nom. Companhia de Seguros Imperio v Heath (REBX) Ltd [2001] 1 W.L.R. 112;
    [2000] 2 All E.R. (Comm) 787; [2000] C.L.C. 1543; [2001] Lloyd's Rep. I.R. 109;
    [2000] Lloyd's Rep. P.N. 795; (2000-01) 3 I.T.E.L.R. 134 4-133
Citco Banking Corp NV v Pusser's Ltd [2007] UKPC 13; [2007] Bus. L.R. 960; [2007]
    B.C.C. 205; [2007] 2 B.C.L.C. 483 5-50
CMS Dolphin Ltd v Simonet [2002] B.C.C. 600; [2001] 2 B.C.L.C. 704; [2001] Emp.
    L.R. 895 4-71
Company (No.002567 of 1982), Re [1983] 1 W.L.R. 927; [1983] 2 All E.R. 854; (1983) 1
    B.C.C. 98930; (1983) 80 L.S.G. 2133; (1983) 127 S.J. 508 Ch D 7-138
Company (No.007623 of 1984), Re (1986) 2 B.C.C. 99191; [1986] B.C.L.C. 362 Ch D
    (Companies Ct) 7-138
Company (No.00477 of 1986), Re (1986) 2 B.C.C. 99171 Ch D 7-138
Company (No.004377 of 1986), Re [1987] 1 W.L.R. 102; [1987] B.C.L.C. 94; (1987) 84
    L.S.G. 653; (1987) 131 S.J. 132 Ch D 7-138
Company (No.002470 of 1988) Ex p. Nicholas, Re [1992] B.C.C. 895 CA (Civ Div) 7-142
Company (No.003102 of 1991) Ex p. Nyckeln Finance Co, Re [1991] B.C.L.C. 539 8-123
Coroin Ltd, Re; sub nom. McKillen v Barclay; McKillen v Misland (Cyprus) Investments
    Ltd [2013] EWCA Civ 781; [2014] B.C.C. 14; [2013] 2 B.C.L.C. 583 .... 3-19, 7-52, 7-99
Coroin, Re [2012] EWHC 521 (Ch) 7-52
Corran v Butters [2017] EWHC 2294 (Ch) 7-202, 8-28
Cosmetic Warriors Ltd v Gerrie [2017] EWCA Civ 324; [2017] 2 B.C.L.C. 456 ...... 3-19, 8-182
Crawley v Short [2009] NSWCA 410; (2009) 76 A.C.S.R. 286 .... 7-106, 11-55
Crossco No.4 Unltd v Jolan Ltd; Jolan Piccadilly Ltd v Piccadilly [2011] EWCA Civ
    1619; [2012] 2 All E.R. 754; [2012] 1 P. & C.R. 16; [2012] 1 E.G.L.R. 137; 14
    I.T.E.L.R. 615 11-58
Crown Dilmun v Sutton [2004] EWHC 52 (Ch); [2004] 1 B.C.L.C. 468; [2004] W.T.L.R.
    497; (2004) 101(7) L.S.G. 34 4-71
Cullen Investments Ltd v Brown [2017] EWHC 2793 (Ch) 4-130
CVC/Opportunity Equity Partners Ltd v Demarco Almeida [2002] UKPC 16; [2002]
    B.C.C. 684; [2002] 2 B.C.L.C. 108 8-158
CY Foundation Group Ltd, Re [2013] HKEC 1209 7-37

TABLE OF CASES

Daniels v Daniels [1978] Ch. 406; [1978] 2 W.L.R. 73; [1978] 2 All E.R. 89; (1977) 121 S.J. 605 Ch D 6-20
Day v Cook [2001] EWCA Civ 592; [2003] B.C.C. 256; [2002] 1 B.C.L.C. 1; [2001] Lloyd's Rep. P.N. 551; [2001] P.N.L.R. 32.. 11-18
DEG-Deutsche Investitions und Entwicklungsgesellschaft mbH v Koshy (Account of Profits: Limitations); sub nom. Gwembe Valley Development Co Ltd (In Receivership) v Koshy (Account of Profits: Limitations) [2003] EWCA Civ 1048; [2004] 1 B.C.L.C. 131; [2004] W.T.L.R. 97; (2003) 147 S.J.L.B. 1086.......................... 4-71, 4-133
Dernacourt Investments Pty Ltd, Re (1990) 2 ACSR 553 7-52
DR Chemicals Ltd, Re (1989) 5 B.C.C. 39 7-138
Dusik v Newton (1985) 62 B.C.L.R. 1 11-55
Ebrahimi v Westbourne Galleries Ltd; sub nom. Westbourne Galleries, Re [1973] A.C. 360; [1972] 2 W.L.R. 1289; [1972] 2 All E.R. 492; (1972) 116 S.J. 412 HL..... 7-37, 7-94, 7-138, 7-142
Edge v Pensions Ombudsman [2000] Ch. 602; [2000] 3 W.L.R. 79; [1999] 4 All E.R. 546; [2000] I.C.R. 748; [1999] O.P.L.R. 179; [1999] Pens. L.R. 215; (1999) 96(35) L.S.G. 39; (1999) 149 N.L.J. 1442 CA (Civ Div) 4-31
Edwardian Group Ltd, Re; sub nom. Estera Trust (Jersey) Ltd v Singh [2018] EWHC 1715 (Ch).... 7-66, 6-67, 7-75, 7-94, 7-99, 7-100, 7-127, 7-142, 7-165, 7-172, 7-202, 7-205, 8-37, 8-91, 8-128, 8-131, 8-158, 8-163, 11-58
Edwardian Group Ltd, Re; sub nom. Estera Trust (Jersey) Ltd v Singh [2017] EWHC 2805 (Ch) 9-37
Electrical Waste Recycling Group Ltd v Philips Electronics UK Ltd [2012] EWHC 38 (Ch)... 9-47
Electricity Generation Corp v Woodside Energy Ltd (2014) 251 C.L.R. 640 HC (Aus) 3-19
Elliott v Planet Organic Ltd; sub nom. Planet Organic Ltd, Re [2000] B.C.C. 610; [2000] 1 B.C.L.C. 366 8-128
Ellis v Property Leeds (UK) Ltd [2002] EWCA Civ 32; [2002] 2 B.C.L.C. 175 11-18
Equity & Provident Ltd, Re [2002] EWHC 186 (Ch); [2002] 2 B.C.L.C. 78 4-71
Estafnous v London & Leeds Business Centres Ltd [2011] EWCA Civ 1157; [2011] 42 E.G. 121 (C.S.); [2012] 1 P. & C.R. DG4... 3-19
Estate Acquisition & Development Ltd, Re [1995] B.C.C. 338 Ch D 7-52
Estmanco (Kilner House) Ltd v Greater London Council [1982] 1 W.L.R. 2; [1982] 1 All E.R. 437; 80 L.G.R. 464; (1981) 125 S.J. 790 6-20
Eurofinance Group Ltd, Re. See Parkinson v Eurofinance Group Ltd 8-158
Exeter City AFC Ltd v Football Conference Ltd [2004] EWHC 831 (Ch); [2004] 1 W.L.R. 2910; [2004] 4 All E.R. 1179; [2004] B.C.C. 498; [2005] 1 B.C.L.C. 238; (2004) 101(9) L.S.G. 31.. 7-198
F&C Alternative Investments (Holdings) Ltd v Barthelemy; Barthelemy v F&C Alternative Investments (Holdings) Ltd; sub nom. F&C Partners LLP, Re [2011] EWHC 1731 (Ch); [2012] Ch. 613; [2012] 3 W.L.R. 10; [2012] Bus. L.R. 891 .... 3-26, 8-37
Falmouth House Freehold Co Ltd, Re; sub nom. Treetop Investment LLC v Falmouth House Freehold Co Ltd [2017] EWHC 674 (Ch)................................... 7-204
Farrar v Miller [2018] EWCA Civ 172; [2018] 2 P. & C.R. DG3 11-58
Fassihi v Item Software (UK) Ltd. See Item Software (UK) Ltd v Fassihi 4-71
Fildes Bros, Re [1970] 1 W.L.R. 592; [1970] 1 All E.R. 923; (1970) 114 S.J. 301 8-30
First Subsea Ltd (formerly BSW Ltd) v Balltec Ltd [2017] EWCA Civ 186; [2018] Ch. 25; [2017] 3 W.L.R. 896; [2018] 1 B.C.L.C. 20; [2017] F.S.R. 37..................... 4-133
Folkes Group Plc v Alexander [2002] EWHC 51 (Ch); [2002] 2 B.C.L.C. 254 3-19
Fort Gilkicker Ltd, Re; sub nom. Universal Project Management Services Ltd v Fort Gilkicker Ltd [2013] EWHC 348 (Ch); [2013] Ch. 551; [2013] 3 W.L.R. 164; [2013] 3 All E.R. 546; [2013] B.C.C. 365; (2013) 163 N.L.J. 268 .... 6-08, 6-20
Fortuna Development Corp, Re [2004-5] CILR 533 10-61
Foss v Harbottle 67 E.R. 189; (1843) 2 Hare 461 Ch 6-08, 6-14, 6-20, 6-22, 11-46, 14-18
Foster Bryant Surveying Ltd v Bryant [2007] EWCA Civ 200; [2007] Bus. L.R. 1565; [2007] B.C.C. 804; [2007] 2 B.C.L.C. 239; [2007] I.R.L.R. 425; [2007] 12 E.G. 154 (C.S.); (2007) 104(13) L.S.G. 24 4-71
Foundry Miniatures Ltd, Re; sub nom. Pinfold v Ansell [2017] EWHC 889 (Ch); [2017] 2 B.C.L.C. 489 .... 7-96, 7-142, 7-153, 7-169, 8-164
Fulham Football Club (1987) Ltd v Richards [2011] EWCA Civ 855; [2012] Ch. 333; [2012] 2 W.L.R. 1008; [2012] 1 All E.R. 414; [2012] 1 All E.R. (Comm) 1148; [2012] Bus. L.R. 606; [2011] B.C.C. 910; [2012] 1 B.C.L.C. 335; [2012] 1 C.L.C. 850; [2011] Arb. L.R. 22 7-198

TABLE OF CASES

Gamatronic (UK) Ltd v Hamilton [2016] EWHC 2225 (QB); [2017] B.C.C. 670 4-71
Gardner v Parker [2004] EWCA Civ 781; [2005] B.C.C. 46; [2004] 2 B.C.L.C. 554;
   (2004) 148 S.J.L.B. 792 11-18
Generator Developments Ltd v Lidl UK GmbH [2018] EWCA Civ 396; [2018] 2 P. &
   C.R. 7; [2018] 2 P. & C.R. DG2.................................. 7-85, 7-94, 11-58
Ghossoub v Team Y&R Holdings Hong Kong Ltd [2016] HKEC 1341 .... 7-198, 7-202
Giles v Rhind (Damages) [2003] EWHC 2830 (Ch); [2004] 1 B.C.L.C. 385 11-20
Giles v Rhind [2002] EWCA Civ 1428; [2003] Ch. 618; [2003] 2 W.L.R. 237; [2002] 4
   All E.R. 977; [2003] B.C.C. 79; [2003] 1 B.C.L.C. 1; (2002) 99(44) L.S.G. 32 ...... 11-18, 11-20
Gillatt v Sky Television Ltd (formerly Sky Television Plc) [2000] 1 All E.R. (Comm) 461;
   [2000] 2 B.C.L.C. 103 CA (Civ Div) 8-131
Goodwin v Cook unreported, 25 June 2018 Ch D 6-51
Grace v Biagioli [2005] EWCA Civ 1222; [2006] B.C.C. 85; [2006] 2 B.C.L.C. 70; (2005)
   102(48) L.S.G. 18 .... 7-202, 8-30
Graham v Every [2014] EWCA Civ 191; [2014] B.C.C. 376; [2015] 1 B.C.L.C. 41 7-52
Gray v Braid Group (Holdings) Ltd [2016] CSIH 68; 2017 S.C. 409; 2016 S.L.T. 1003;
   2017 S.C.L.R. 599; 2016 G.W.D. 29-517................... 7-194, 7-202, 8-18, 8-173
Griffin v Wainwright unreported, 18 August 2017 Ch D 8-178
Gross v Rackind; sub nom. Citybranch Group Ltd, Re; City Branch Group Ltd, Re;
   Rackind v Gross [2004] EWCA Civ 815; [2005] 1 W.L.R. 3505; [2004] 4 All E.R. 735;
   [2005] B.C.C. 11; (2004) 148 S.J.L.B. 661 7-52
Guidezone Ltd, Re; Kaneria v Kaneria [2014] EWHC 1165 (Ch); [2014] 1 W.L.R. 3728;
   [2014] 3 Costs L.R. 554 7-94
Guidezone Ltd, Re; sub nom. Kaneria v Patel [2001] B.C.C. 692; [2000] 2 B.C.L.C. 321
   Ch D (Companies Ct) 7-85, 7-113
Gwembe Valley Development Co Ltd (In Receivership) v Koshy (Account of Profits:
   Limitations). *See* DEG-Deutsche Investitions und Entwicklungsgesellschaft mbH v
   Koshy (Account of Profits: Limitations) 4-71, 4-133
Hailey Group, Re; sub nom. Company (No.008126 of 1989), Re [1992] B.C.C. 542;
   [1993] B.C.L.C. 459 Ch D (Companies Ct)...................................... 8-30
Halt Garage (1964) Ltd, Re [1982] 3 All E.R. 1016 Ch D 7-153
Hanspaul v Ward [2016] EWHC 1358 (Ch) 8-97
Hanspaul v Ward unreported, 9 March 2017 8-97
Harbour Front Ltd v Leung Yuet Keung [2018] HKEC 334 HKCFI 7-202
Harris v Microfusion 2003-2 LLP; sub nom. Microfusion 2003-2 LLP v Harris [2016]
   EWCA Civ 1212; [2017] C.P. Rep. 15; [2017] 1 B.C.L.C. 305 .. 6-08, 6-20, 6-22, 6-23, 6-36, 6-74,
   6-74
Harris v Microfusion 2003-2 LLP; sub nom. Microfusion 2003-2 LLP v Harris [2016]
   EWCA Civ 1212; [2017] C.P. Rep. 15; [2017] 1 B.C.L.C. 305....................... 14-18
Hawkes v Cuddy; sub nom. Neath Rugby Ltd, Re [2009] EWCA Civ 291; [2010] B.C.C.
   597; [2009] 2 B.C.L.C. 427 7-52
Haysport Properties Ltd v Ackerman [2016] EWHC 393 (Ch); [2016] B.C.C. 676; [2016]
   2 B.C.L.C. 522 4-133
Hedger v Adams; sub nom. Pro4Sport Ltd (In Liquidation), Re [2015] EWHC 2540 (Ch);
   [2016] B.C.C. 390; [2016] 1 B.C.L.C. 257.. 4-20
Henderson PFI Secondary Fund II LLP v Henderson PFI Secondary Fund II LP. *See*
   Certain Ltd Partners in Henderson PFI Secondary Fund II LLP v Henderson PFI
   Secondary Fund II LP 6-22
Henderson v Henderson [1843-60] All E.R. Rep. 378; 67 E.R. 313; (1843) 3 Hare 100 Ch ... 7-204
Highfield Commodities Ltd, Re [1985] 1 W.L.R. 149; [1984] 3 All E.R. 884; (1984) 1
   B.C.C. 99277; [1985] P.C.C. 191; (1984) 81 L.S.G. 3589; (1984) 128 S.J. 870 Ch D 8-123
Hillsdown Holdings Plc v Pensions Ombudsman [1997] 1 All E.R. 862; [1996] O.P.L.R.
   291; [1996] Pens. L.R. 427... 4-31
HLC Environmental Projects Ltd, Re; sub nom. Hellard v De Brito Carvalho [2013]
   EWHC 2876 (Ch); [2014] B.C.C. 337 4-20
HSBC Bank Middle East v Clarke [2006] UKPC 31 3-19
Humberclyde Finance Group Ltd v Hicks unreported 4 November 2001 Ch D 11-18
Hunter Kane Ltd v Watkins [2003] EWHC 186 (Ch) 4-717
Iesini v Westrip Holdings Ltd [2009] EWHC 2526 (Ch); [2010] B.C.C. 420; [2011] 1
   B.C.L.C. 498.. 6-08
In Plus Group Ltd v Pyke [2002] EWCA Civ 370; [2003] B.C.C. 332; [2002] 2 B.C.L.C.
   201... 4-71

TABLE OF CASES

Interactive Technology Corp Ltd v Ferster; sub nom. Ferster v Ferster [2016] EWHC 2896 (Ch) 7-202
International Leisure Ltd v First National Trustee Co UK Ltd [2012] EWHC 1971 (Ch); [2013] Ch. 346; [2013] 2 W.L.R. 466; [2012] B.C.C. 738; [2014] 1 B.C.L.C. 128; [2012] P.N.L.R. 34 11-18
Irvine v Irvine [2006] EWHC 406 (Ch); [2007] 1 B.C.L.C. 349 .... 7-153, 8-158
Island Holdings Ltd v Birchington Engineering Co Ltd unreported, 7 July 1981 11-58
Item Software (UK) Ltd v Fassihi; sub nom. Fassihi v Item Software (UK) Ltd [2004] EWCA Civ 1244; [2004] B.C.C. 994; [2005] 2 B.C.L.C. 91; [2005] I.C.R. 450; [2004] I.R.L.R. 928; (2004) 101(39) L.S.G. 34; (2004) 148 S.J.L.B. 1153..................... 4-71
Jackson v Dear; sub nom. Dear v Jackson [2013] EWCA Civ 89; [2014] 1 B.C.L.C. 18 3-19
Jas Financial Products LLP v Icap Plc [2017] EWHC 1172 (Comm) 11-86
JD Wetherspoon Plc v Van De Berg & Co Ltd [2007] EWHC 1044 (Ch); [2007] P.N.L.R. 28. 4-133
Jenkins v Supascaf [2006] 3 N.Z.L.R. 264 8-30
JJ Harrison (Properties) Ltd v Harrison [2001] EWCA Civ 1467; [2002] B.C.C. 729; [2002] 1 B.C.L.C. 162; [2001] W.T.L.R. 1327.. 4-133
John Alexander's Clubs Pty Ltd v White City Tennis Club Ltd [2010] 241 C.L.R. 1 HCA ... 11-58, 11-69
Johnson v Gore Wood & Co (No.1); Johnson v Gore Woods & Co [2002] 2 A.C. 1; [2001] 2 W.L.R. 72; [2001] 1 All E.R. 481; [2001] C.P.L.R. 49; [2001] B.C.C. 820; [2001] 1 B.C.L.C. 313; [2001] P.N.L.R. 18; (2001) 98(1) L.S.G. 24; (2001) 98(8) L.S.G. 46; (2000) 150 N.L.J. 1889; (2001) 145 S.J.L.B. 29 11-20
Joiner v George [2002] EWCA Civ 160; [2003] B.C.C. 298 8-128
Julien v Evolving TecKnologies and Enterprise Development Co Ltd [2018] UKPC 2; [2018] B.C.C. 376. 4-133
Kaye v Croydon Tramways Co [1898] 1 Ch. 358 CA 5-23
Khoshkhou v Cooper [2014] EWHC 1087 (Ch) 7-85
Kilcarne Holdings Ltd v Targetfollow (Birmingham) Ltd [2005] EWCA Civ 1355; [2005] N.P.C. 132; [2006] 1 P. & C.R. DG20. 11-58
Lai Chi Keung v Wang Zhihua [2018] HKEC 1004 8-01
Latin American Investments Ltd v Maroil Trading Inc; Oceanic Trans Shipping Corp v Maroil Trading Inc [2017] EWHC 1254 (Comm) 11-18
LCM Wealth Management Ltd, Re; sub nom. Moxon v Litchfield [2013] EWHC 3957 (Ch). 7-194
Leeds United Holdings Plc, Re [1997] B.C.C. 131; [1996] 2 B.C.L.C. 545 Ch D 7-52
Legal Costs Negotiators Ltd, Re; sub nom. Morris v Hateley [1999] B.C.C. 547; [1999] 2 B.C.L.C. 171; (1999) 96(13) L.S.G. 31 CA (Civ Div)................................. 7-52
Li Guozhu v New Century Iatrical Inv Management Ltd [2018] HKEC 1021 7-52
Lim Kok Wah v Lim Boh Yong [2015] SGHC 211 .... 7-37, 7-40, 7-94
Links Golf Tasmania v Sattler [2012] F.C.A. 634 4-71
Lion Nathan v Coopers [2006] F.C.A.F.C. 144 3-19
London School of Electronics Ltd, Re [1986] Ch. 211; [1985] 3 W.L.R. 474; (1985) 1 B.C.C. 99394; [1985] P.C.C. 248; (1985) 129 S.J. 573 Ch D........................ 7-202
Lungowe v Vedanta Resources Plc [2017] EWCA Civ 1528; [2018] 1 W.L.R. 3575; [2017] B.C.C. 787; [2017] B.L.R. 585 .... 11-12, 12-27
Macquarie International Health Clinic Pty Ltd v Sydney South West Area Health Service [2010] NSWCA 268 3-26
Malhotra v Malhotra [2014] EWHC 113 (Comm); [2015] 1 B.C.L.C. 428 11-18
Marks & Spencer Plc v BNP Paribas Securities Services Trust Co (Jersey) Ltd [2015] UKSC 72; [2016] A.C. 742; [2015] 3 W.L.R. 1843; [2016] 4 All E.R. 441; 163 Con. L.R. 1; [2016] 1 P. & C.R. 13; [2016] L. & T.R. 8; [2016] C.I.L.L. 3779 3-19
Masood v Zahoor [2009] EWCA Civ 650; [2010] 1 W.L.R. 746; [2010] 1 All E.R. 888; [2009] C.P. Rep. 44; [2010] Bus. L.R. D12 7-204
McEneaney v Stevens unreported, 2 May 2017 Ch D 6-14
McLoughlin v Grovers; sub nom. McLoughlin v Jones; McCloughlin v Grovers [2001] EWCA Civ 1743; [2002] Q.B. 1312; [2002] 2 W.L.R. 1279; [2002] P.I.Q.R. P20; [2002] P.N.L.R. 21 9-49
Mediterranean Salvage & Towage Ltd v Seamar Trading & Commerce Inc (The Reborn) [2009] EWCA Civ 531; [2010] 1 All E.R. (Comm) 1; [2009] 2 Lloyd's Rep. 639; [2009] 1 C.L.C. 909; (2009) 159 N.L.J. 898 3-19
Messih v McMillan Williams [2010] EWCA Civ 844; [2010] C.P. Rep. 41; [2010] 6 Costs L.R. 914 8-97

TABLE OF CASES

Meyer v Scottish Cooperative Wholesale Society Ltd; sub nom. Scottish Cooperative Wholesale Society v Meyer; Meyer v Scottish Textile & Manufacturing Co Ltd [1959] A.C. 324; [1958] 3 W.L.R. 404; [1958] 3 All E.R. 66; 1958 S.C. (H.L.) 40; 1958 S.L.T. 241; (1958) 102 S.J. 617 7-52
Micra Contracts Ltd (In Liquidation), Re; sub nom. Fox v Bishop [2016] B.C.C. 153 4-68
Movitex v Bulfield (1986) 2 B.C.C. 99403; [1988] B.C.L.C. 104 Ch D 4-31
Murad v Al-Saraj; Murad v Westwood Business Inc [2005] EWCA Civ 959; [2005] W.T.L.R. 1573; (2005) 102(32) L.S.G. 31 .... 4-31, 4-71
Neath Rugby Ltd, Re. *See* Hawkes v Cuddy 7-52
Nelson's Yard Management Co v Eziefula [2013] EWCA Civ 235; [2013] C.P. Rep. 29; [2013] B.L.R. 289; [2013] 14 E.G. 87 (C.S.) 8-97
Neptune (Vehicle Washing Equipment) Ltd v Fitzgerald (No.2) [1995] B.C.C. 1000 4-71
New Zealand Netherlands Society "Oranjer" v Kuys; sub nom. New Zealand Netherlands Society Oranje Inc v Kuys [1973] 1 W.L.R. 1126; [1973] 2 All E.R. 1222; [1974] R.P.C. 272; (1973) 117 S.J. 565 PC (NZ) 4-71
Newgate Stud Co v Penfold [2004] EWHC 2993 (Ch); [2008] 1 B.C.L.C. 46 4-71
Northampton Regional Livestock Centre Co Ltd v Cowling [2015] EWCA Civ 651; [2016] 1 B.C.L.C. 431; [2015] 4 Costs L.O. 477; [2016] P.N.L.R. 5 4-71
O'Neill v Phillips; sub nom. Company (No.709 of 1992), Re; Pectel Ltd, Re [1999] 1 W.L.R. 1092; [1999] 2 All E.R. 961; [1999] B.C.C. 600; [1999] 2 B.C.L.C. 1; (1999) 96(23) L.S.G. 33; (1999) 149 N.L.J. 805 HL 7-37, 7-94, 7-113, 7-138, 8-91, 11-58
Oak Investment Partners XII Ltd Partnership v Boughtwood; sub nom. Boughtwood v Oak Investment Partners XII Ltd Partnership [2010] EWCA Civ 23; [2010] 2 B.C.L.C. 459 7-106
One Step (Support) Ltd v Morris-Garner; sub nom. Morris-Garner v One Step (Support) Ltd [2016] EWCA Civ 180; [2017] Q.B. 1; [2016] 3 W.L.R. 1281; [2017] 2 All E.R. 262; [2016] I.R.L.R. 435 4-71
OS3 Distribution Ltd, Re; sub nom. Watchstone Group Plc v Quob Park Estate Ltd [2017] EWHC 2621 (Ch) 7-74
Over & Over Ltd v Bonvests Holdings Ltd [2010] SGCA 7 .... 7-37, 4-40
Overlook v Foxtel [2002] NSWSC 17 3-26
Owens v Owens [2018] UKSC 41; [2018] 3 W.L.R. 634; [2018] 2 F.C.R. 796 2-21
Owusu v Jackson (t/a Villa Holidays Bal Inn Villas) (C-281/02) EU:C:2005:120; [2005] Q.B. 801; [2005] 2 W.L.R. 942; [2005] 2 All E.R. (Comm) 577; [2005] 1 Lloyd's Rep. 452; [2005] E.C.R. I-1383; [2005] 1 C.L.C. 246; [2005] I.L.Pr. 25 12-27
Pallant v Morgan [1953] Ch. 43; [1952] 2 All E.R. 951; [1952] 2 T.L.R. 813 Ch D 11-58
Palmer v Loveland unreported, 16 August 2017 8-126
Parkinson v Eurofinance Group Ltd; sub nom. Eurofinance Group Ltd, Re [2001] B.C.C. 551; [2001] 1 B.C.L.C. 720; (2000) 97(27) L.S.G. 37 Ch D 8-158
Peak Hotel and Resorts Ltd v Tarek Investments Ltd [2015] EWHC 3048 (Ch) 11-18, 11-20
Pedersen (Thameside) Ltd, Re; sub nom. Mewslade Holdings Ltd v Gourgey [2017] EWHC 3406 (Ch); [2018] B.C.C. 58 8-35
Percival v Wright [1902] 2 Ch. 421 Ch D 11-46
Perry v Day [2004] EWHC 3372 (Ch); [2005] 2 B.C.L.C. 405 11-18
Persad v Singh [2017] UKPC 32; [2017] B.C.C. 779; [2018] 1 P. & C.R. DG6 11-80
Peskin v Anderson [2001] B.C.C. 874; [2001] 1 B.C.L.C. 372 CA (Civ Div) 11-46
Petrodel Resources Ltd v Prest; sub nom. Prest v Petrodel Resources Ltd; P Resources Ltd v Prest; Prest v Prest [2013] UKSC 34; [2013] 2 A.C. 415; [2013] 3 W.L.R. 1; [2013] 4 All E.R. 673; [2013] B.C.C. 571; [2014] 1 B.C.L.C. 30; [2013] 2 F.L.R. 732; [2013] 3 F.C.R. 210; [2013] W.T.L.R. 1249; [2013] Fam. Law 953; (2013) 163(7565) N.L.J. 27; (2013) 157(24) S.J.L.B. 37 11-80
Pinfold v Ansell. *See* Foundry Miniatures Ltd, Re 7-96, 7-142, 7-153, 7-169, 8-164
Planet Organic Ltd, Re. *See* Elliott v Planet Organic Ltd 8-128
Playboy Club London Ltd v Banca Nazionale del Lavoro SpA [2018] UKSC 43; [2018] 1 W.L.R. 4041 11-27
PM Law Ltd v Motorplus Ltd [2018] EWCA Civ 1730 3-19
Poon Ka Man Mason v Cheng Wai Tao (2016) 19 HKCFAR 144 .... 4-31, 4-68, 4-83, 4-93
Premier Electronics (GB) Ltd, Re; sub nom. Pickering v Lynch [2002] B.C.C. 911; [2002] 2 B.C.L.C. 634 Ch D 8-126
Prudential Assurance Co Ltd v Newman Industries Ltd [1982] Ch. 204; [1982] 2 W.L.R. 31; [1982] 1 All E.R. 354 CA (Civ Div) 11-46
Quarter Master UK Ltd (In Liquidation) v Pyke [2004] EWHC 1815 (Ch); [2005] 1 B.C.L.C. 245 4-71

TABLE OF CASES xvii

RA Noble (Clothing) Ltd [1983] B.C.L.C. 273 .... 7-138, 7-142
RAC Motoring Services Ltd, Re; sub nom. Royal Automobile Club Ltd, Re [2000] 1
   B.C.L.C. 307 5-23
Rackind v Gross. *See* Gross v Rackind 7-52
Rainy Sky SA v Kookmin Bank; sub nom. Kookmin Bank v Rainy Sky SA [2011] UKSC
   50; [2011] 1 W.L.R. 2900; [2012] 1 All E.R. 1137; [2012] 1 All E.R. (Comm) 1; [2012]
   Bus. L.R. 313; [2012] 1 Lloyd's Rep. 34; [2011] 2 C.L.C. 923; [2012] B.L.R. 132; 138
   Con. L.R. 1; [2011] C.I.L.L. 3105 3-19
Rembert v Daniel [2018] EWHC 388 (Ch); [2018] 2 B.C.L.C. 156 8-14
Residues Treatment & Trading Co Ltd v Southern Resources Ltd (1988) 14 A.C.L.R. 375 5-23
Revenue and Customs Commissioners v Egleton [2006] EWHC 2313 (Ch); [2006]
   EWHC 2313 (Ch); [2007] 1 All E.R. 606; [2007] Bus. L.R. 44; [2007] B.C.C. 78;
   [2006] S.T.I. 2233; (2006) 103(38) L.S.G. 35; (2006) 150 S.J.L.B. 1252 8-126
Revenue and Customs Commissioners v Rochdale Drinks Distributors Ltd [2011] EWCA
   Civ 1116; [2012] S.T.C. 186; [2013] B.C.C. 419; [2012] 1 B.C.L.C. 748; [2011]
   B.P.I.R. 1604; [2011] S.T.I. 2776 8-123
Richardson v Blackmore; Capital Cabs Ltd v Blackmore [2005] EWCA Civ 1356; [2006]
   B.C.C. 276 7-202
Roadchef (Employees Benefits Trustees) Ltd v Ingram Hill [2013] EWHC 939 (Ch) 9-47
Rotadata Ltd, Re [2000] B.C.C. 686; [2000] 1 B.C.L.C. 122 Ch D (Companies Ct) 9-47
Salomon v Salomon & Co Ltd [1897] A.C. 22 HL 11-46
Saul D Harrison & Sons Plc, Re [1994] B.C.C. 475; [1995] 1 B.C.L.C. 14 CA 7-138
Scottish Cooperative Wholesale Society v Meyer. *See* Meyer v Scottish Cooperative
   Wholesale Society Ltd 7-52
Scottish Widows Fund and Life Assurance Society v BGC International (formerly Cantor
   Fitzgerald International) [2012] EWCA Civ 607; 142 Con. L.R. 27 3-19
SDI Retail Services Ltd v King [2017] EWHC 737 (Ch) 3-19, 6-26, 6-43, 6-51, 6-60
Sevilleja Garcia v Marex Financial Ltd [2018] EWCA Civ 1468 .... 11-18, 11-20
Sharp v Blank [2015] EWHC 3220 (Ch); [2017] B.C.C. 187 .... 5-23, 7-106, 11-46, 11-55
Sheikh v Ijaz [2018] EWHC 1693 (Ch) 7-142
Shepherds Investments Ltd v Walters [2006] EWHC 836 (Ch); [2007] 2 B.C.L.C. 202;
   [2007] I.R.L.R. 110; [2007] F.S.R. 15; (2006) 150 S.J.L.B. 536 4-71
Shih Hua Investment Co Ltd v Zhang Aidong [2017] HKEC 88 8-114
Sigma Finance Corp (In Administration), Re [2009] UKSC 2; [2010] 1 All E.R. 571;
   [2010] B.C.C. 40; (2009) 159 N.L.J. 1550; (2009) 153(42) S.J.L.B. 29 3-19
Singularis Holdings Ltd (In Official Liquidation) v Daiwa Capital Markets Europe Ltd
   [2018] EWCA Civ 84; [2018] 1 W.L.R. 2777; [2018] Bus. L.R. 1115; [2018] 1 Lloyd's
   Rep. 472; [2018] 2 B.C.L.C. 1; [2018] P.N.L.R. 19 .... 4-20, 11-85
Sivagnanam v Barclays Bank Plc [2015] EWHC 3985 (Comm) 11-18
St Vincent European General Partner Ltd v Robinson [2018] EWHC 1230 (Comm) .. 11-18, 11-20
Stainer v Lee [2010] EWHC 1539 (Ch); [2011] B.C.C. 134; [2011] 1 B.C.L.C. 537 .... 6-43, 6-51
Staray Capital Ltd v Yang (aka Stanley) [2017] UKPC 43 .... 5-46, 5-50
Stein v Blake (No.2) [1998] 1 All E.R. 724; [1998] B.C.C. 316; [1998] 1 B.C.L.C. 573 11-46
Stena Line Ltd v Merchant Navy Ratings Pension Fund Trustees Ltd; sub nom. Stena Line
   Ltd v MNRPF Trustees Ltd [2011] EWCA Civ 543; [2011] Pens. L.R. 223 3-19
Strahan v Wilcock [2006] EWCA Civ 13; [2006] B.C.C. 320; [2006] 2 B.C.L.C. 555;
   (2006) 103(6) L.S.G. 30 CA (Civ Div) 8-158
Streeter v Western Areas Exploration (No.2) [2011] WASCA 17 4-71
Sukhoruchkin v Van Bekestein [2013] EWHC 1993 (Ch) 11-18
Summers v Fairclough Homes Ltd; sub nom. Fairclough Homes Ltd v Summers [2012]
   UKSC 26; [2012] 1 W.L.R. 2004; [2012] 4 All E.R. 317; [2012] 4 Costs L.R. 760;
   [2013] Lloyd's Rep. I.R. 159; (2012) 162 N.L.J. 910; (2012) 156(26) S.J.L.B. 31 7-204
Sunrise Radio Ltd, Re; sub nom. Kohli v Avtar Lit [2011] EWHC 3821 (Ch) 8-128, 8-158
Tiessen v Henderson [1899] 1 Ch. 861 Ch D 5-23
TPD Investments Ltd, Re; sub nom. Destiny Investments (1993) Ltd v TH Holdings Ltd
   TH Holdings Ltd (Formerly Tonstate (Hotels) Ltd) v Destiny Investments (1993)
   Ltd[2017] EWHC 657 (Ch) 8-37, 8-48, 8-159
Tremendous Success Holdings Ltd v Sinosoft Technology Group Ltd [2016] HKEC 1509 6-22
Ultraframe (UK) Ltd v Fielding; Burnden Group Plc v Northstar Systems Ltd (In
   Liquidation); Northstar Systems Ltd (In Liquidation) v Fielding [2005] EWHC 1638
   (Ch); [2006] F.S.R. 17; [2007] W.T.L.R. 835; (2005) 28(9) I.P.D. 28069 .... 4-31, 4-71
Union Accident Insurance Co, Re [1972] 1 All E.R. 1105; [1972] 1 Lloyd's Rep. 297;
   (1971) 116 S.J. 274 8-123

Unisoft Group Ltd (No.3), Re; sub nom. Unisoft Group Ltd (No.2), Re [1994] B.C.C. 766; [1994] 1 B.C.L.C. 609 7-52
Valastiak v Valastiak [2010] BCCA71 11-55
VB Football Assets v Blackpool Football Club (Properties) Ltd (formerly Segesta Ltd) [2017] EWHC 2767 (Ch) 7-37, 7-85, 7-94, 7-113, 8-29, 9-47, 11-58
Waddington Ltd v Chan Chun Hoo Thomas [2009] 2 B.C.L.C. 82 11-18
Wann v Birkinshaw [2017] EWCA Civ 84 .... 8-128, 8-136, 8-158, 8-159
Watercor Ltd, Re; sub nom. Edgar v Munro [2017] EWHC 1814 (Ch) 8-134, 8-164
Webster v Sandersons Solicitors [2009] EWCA Civ 830; [2009] 2 B.C.L.C. 542; [2009] P.N.L.R. 37; [2010] Pens. L.R. 169; (2009) 106(32) L.S.G. 15 11-18
Whillock v Henderson [2007] CSOH 175; 2007 S.L.T. 1222; [2009] B.C.C. 314; 2007 G.W.D. 38-663 7-52
Wilkinson v West Coast Capital [2005] EWHC 3009 (Ch); [2007] B.C.C. 717 4-71
Williams v Central Bank of Nigeria; sub nom. Central Bank of Nigeria v Williams [2014] UKSC 10; [2014] A.C. 1189; [2014] 2 W.L.R. 355; [2014] 2 All E.R. 489; [2014] W.T.L.R. 873; 16 I.T.E.L.R. 740; (2014) 164(7596) N.L.J. 16 4-133
Wilton UK Ltd v Shuttleworth [2018] EWHC 911 (Ch) 6-78
Winchester Park Ltd v Sehayak [2016] EWHC 1216 (QB) 8-97
Wood v Sureterm Direct Ltd; sub nom. Wood v Capita Insurance Services Ltd [2017] UKSC 24; [2017] A.C. 1173; [2017] 2 W.L.R. 1095; [2017] 4 All E.R. 615; [2018] 1 All E.R. (Comm) 51; 171 Con. L.R. 1; [2017] C.I.L.L. 3971 3-19
Woolwich v Milne; Woolwich v Twenty Twenty Productions [2003] EWHC 414 (Ch) 7-142
Wootliff v Rushton-Turner [2016] EWHC 2802 (Ch); [2018] 1 B.C.L.C. 48 7-142
Wootliff v Rushton-Turner [2017] EWHC 3129 (Ch); [2018] 1 B.C.L.C. 479 7-96
Yam Seng Pte Ltd v International Trade Corp Ltd [2013] EWHC 111 (QB); [2013] 1 All E.R. (Comm) 1321; [2013] 1 Lloyd's Rep. 526; [2013] 1 C.L.C. 662; [2013] B.L.R. 147; 146 Con. L.R. 39; [2013] Bus. L.R. D53 3-26
Yung Yui Kwai v Yung Woon Kwai [2017] HKEC 2824 .... 8-168, 9-32
Zavahir v Shankleman [2016] EWHC 2772 (Ch); [2017] B.C.C. 500 .... 6-48, 6-61

TABLE OF STATUTES

1948	Companies Act 1948 (c.38)
	s.210 7-138
1980	Companies Act 1980 (c.22)
	s.75 7-52
1980	Limitation Act 1980 (c.58)
	s.21 4-133
	(1)(a) 4-133
	(b) 4-133
	s.32 4-133
	(1)(b) 4-133
	(2) 4-133
1985	Companies Act 1985 (c.6)
	s.459 7-52
1986	Insolvency Act 1986 (c.45)
	s.135 8-123
2001	Corporations Act 2001 (Cth)
	s.9 9-32
	s.247A 9-32
2006	Companies Act 2006 (c.46) 9-30
	Pt 11 6-23
	s.22(2) 3-62
	(3)(b) 3-62
	s.116 et seq 5-23
	s.175(1) 4-71
	(4)(a) 4-71
	ss.175—177 4-71
	s.176(4) 4-71
	s.177(6)(a) 4-71
	s.260(1) 6-08
	s.263(3)(f) 6-60
	s.320 7-52
	s.994 .. 6-60, 7-202, 7-204, 8-01, 8-30, 8-126, 9-30
	(1) 7-52
	ss.994—996 .... 6-08, 7-198
	s.996 .... 7-205, 8-14
2011	Charity Act 2011 (c.25) 5-31
2012	Cayman Islands Companies Law (2012 Revision) 2012
	s.104 8-123

TABLE OF STATUTORY INSTRUMENTS

1998 Civil Procedure Rules 1998 (SI 1998/3132) . 7-204, 8-97, 9-30, 9-47
    r.3.5 9-30
    Pt 7 PD 10-08, 10-61
2009 Companies (Unfair Prejudice Applications) Proceedings Rules 2009 (SI 2009/2469) 9-30
    r.2(2) 9-30
2016 Insolvency (England and Wales) Rules 2016 (SI 2016/1024)
    rr.7.25—7.36 10-58

CHAPTER 2

Broad Principles

TABLE OF CONTENTS

Separate Legal Personality	2-04
Principle 1—company as a creation of statute	2-04
Principle 2—separate legal personality and lifting the veil	2-05
Principle 3—personal rights of individual shareholder	2-06
The Bargain Between Shareholders	2-07
Principle 4—freedom of contract	2-07
Principle 5—the bargain between shareholders	2-08
Principle 6—directors' duties	2-09
Principle 7—shareholders' control	2-10
Principle 8—majority rule	2-11
Principle 9—voting rights as property	2-12
The Rule in Foss v Harbottle—The Derivative Claim and Constraints in Equity	2-13
Principle 10—the proper claimant	2-14
Principle 11—internal management rule	2-15
Principle 12—exception to Principle 10: the derivative claim	2-16
Principle 13—equitable doctrine of "fraud on the minority"	2-17
Statutory Remedies for the Protection of Minority Shareholders	2-18
Principle 14—the unfair prejudice remedy	2-19
Principle 15—just and equitable	2-20
Principle 16—equitable principles	2-21■

STATUTORY REMEDIES FOR THE PROTECTION OF MINORITY SHAREHOLDERS

PRINCIPLE 16—EQUITABLE PRINCIPLES

After "through them undeterred".", add:

2-21 In relation to Principle 16(1), and the adaptability of equity to changes in social and commercial norms, it may be observed that even the application of a statute (necessarily of fixed "meaning") to the facts of a case can change as social norms change: see *Owens v Owens* [2018] UKSC 41 at [30]–[32]

CHAPTER 3

The Bargain between Shareholders

TABLE OF CONTENTS

Principle 4—freedom of contract	3-01
Principle 5—the bargain between shareholders	3-02
Principle 11—the internal management rule	3-03
Principle 16—equitable principles	3-04
Freedom of Contract	3-15
Construction and Implied Terms	3-16■
The Special Incidents of the Contract Contained in the Articles of Association	3-31
A Collateral Shareholders' Agreement	3-53■
Entrenchment of Rights of Individual Shareholders	3-61■
Class Rights	3-66

CONSTRUCTION AND IMPLIED TERMS

Exclusion of some extrinsic evidence in the interpretation of articles of association

To the end of the paragraph, add:
   The decision of Hildyard J in *Re Beppler & Jacobson Ltd* [2016] EWHC 20 (Ch) was reversed on appeal to the Court of Appeal: [2018] EWCA Civ 763 (on 16 July 2018 the Supreme Court refused permission to appeal).   **3-18**

Ordinary principles of contract law

Replace first paragraph with:
   Apart from the special rules relating to the admissibility of extrinsic evidence, ordinary principles of construction and the implication of terms of contract law in general apply to articles of association: *Folkes Group Plc v Alexander* [2002] 2 B.C.L.C. 254.[5] Indeed, a modern leading (if controversial) case on the construction of contracts and the implication of terms was concerned with the articles of association of a company: *Attorney General of Belize v Belize Telecom* [2009] 1 W.L.R. 1988. That decision now needs to be read in the light of *Arnold v Britton* [2015] A.C. 1619 and *Marks & Spencer Plc v BNP Paribas Securities Services Trust Co (Jersey) Ltd* [2016] A.C. 742, which together survey the plethora of authority in this area.[6] In *Cosmetic Warriors Ltd v Gerrie* [2017] EWCA Civ 324, upholding [2015] EWHC 3718 (Ch), the Court of Appeal, in construing articles of association, observed that the Supreme Court in *Wood v Capita Insurance Services Ltd* [2017] A.C. 1173 confirmed that the principles stated in *Arnold v Britton* did not involve any departure from *Rainy Sky v Kookmin Bank*. In contrast to a sharehold-   **3-19**

ers' agreement, there is a presumption in construing articles of association in favour of freedom to transfer shares: see *United Co Rusal Plc v Crispian Investments Ltd* [2018] EWHC 2415 (Comm) at [42]–[52].

[5] See also *Lion Nathan v Coopers* [2006] F.C.A.F.C. 144 (Federal Court of Australia); *HSBC Bank Middle East v Clarke* [2006] UKPC 31.

[6] For example, *Mediterranean Salvage & Towage Ltd v Seamar Trading & Commerce Inc* [2009] 2 Lloyd's Rep. 639; *Re Sigma Finance Corp* [2010] B.C.C. 40; the judgment of Arden LJ in *Stena Line Ltd v Merchant Navy Ratings Pension Fund Trustees Ltd* [2011] Pens. L.R. 223 at [36]–[41]; *Rainy Sky SA v Kookmin Bank* [2011] 1 W.L.R. 2900; *Estafnous v London & Leeds Business Centres Ltd* [2011] 42 E.G. 121 (C.S.); *Re Coroin Ltd* [2014] B.C.C. 14; *Jackson v Dear* [2014] 1 B.C.L.C. 186. See *Electricity Generation Corp v Woodside Energy Ltd* (2014) 251 C.L.R. 640 (High Court of Australia), in which the English authorities were considered.

After the first paragraph, add new paragraph:

In *SDI Retail Services Ltd v King* [2017] EWHC 737 (Ch) at [58], Richard Millett QC, sitting as a Deputy High Judge, gave this pithy summary of the recent cases in the Supreme Court on the right approach to the construction of contracts:

> "What this means in simple terms is that the court must balance literalism, factual background and common sense in equal measure as best it can."

In *PM Law Ltd v Motorplus Ltd* [2018] EWCA Civ 1730 Asplin LJ gave this summary:

> "It is common ground that the court's task when construing clause 1 of the 2007 Agreement is to ascertain the objective meaning of the words used by the parties in the context of the 2007 Agreement as a whole, taking into account the relevant factual background which would have been available to the parties, but excluding subjective evidence of the parties' intentions. The court must focus on the meaning of the relevant words in their documentary, factual and commercial context. If there is an ambiguity, or in other words, there are rival meanings, the court can give weight to the implications of the rival constructions by reaching a view as to which is more consistent with business common sense: *Arnold v Britton & Ors* [2015] AC 1619 per Lord Neuberger PSC at [14] – [23] and *Wood v Capita Insurance Services Limited* [2017] AC 1173: [2017] UKSC 24 per Lord Hodge JSC at [8] – [15]."

For recent decisions on admissibility of pre-contract negotiations, see *Barclays Bank Plc v Landgraf* [2014] EWHC 503 Comm, in which Popplewell J said "regard could be had to the parties' negotiations for the purpose of determining the genesis and object of a contractual provision", but not referring to *Scottish Widows Fund and Life Assurance Society v BGC International* [2012] EWCA Civ 607, where Arden LJ (as she then was) said:

> "Pre-contractual negotiations rarely descend into detail on every point; the negotiations are unlikely to throw any light on the detailed points of interpretation that generally arise after execution. However this does not necessarily mean that the pre-contractual negotiations should be accepted as evidence even as to the general object of the transaction. Statements made in the course of negotiations are often no more than statements of a negotiating stance at that point in time, thus shedding more heat than light on issues as to interpretation of the final deal."

She concluded that

> "judges should exercise considerable caution before treating as admissible communications in the course of pre-contractual negotiations relied on as evidencing the parties' objective aim in completing the transaction" .

A contractual duty of good faith

Express term

Replace first paragraph with:
In *F&C Alternative Investments v Barthelemy* [2012] Ch. 613, Sales J held (at [252]) that an express contractual duty of "the utmost good faith ... is a form of contractual duty which requires the obligor to have regard to the interests of the obligee, while also being entitled to have regard to its own self-interest when acting". He relied upon the decision of the New South Wales Court of Appeal in *Macquarie International Health Clinic Pty Ltd v Sydney South West Area Health Service* [2010] NSWCA 268. The case concerned the operation of heads of agreement (HOA) between Macquarie and its holding company (MHC) and the respondent (Area Health) which related to the development of a private hospital on land owned by Area Health. The HOA contained contractual obligations for the parties to act with utmost good faith in their dealings with each other. Regarding the content of those obligations, Hodgson JA said, at [146]–[148]:

3-26

> "146. Writing extra-curially, Sir Anthony Mason has argued that a contractual obligation of good faith embraces no less than three related notions: (1) An obligation on the parties to co-operate in achieving the contractual objects; (2) Compliance with honest standards of conduct; and (3) Compliance with standards of conduct that are reasonable having regard to the interests of the parties. See A F Mason "Contract, Good Faith and Equitable Standards in Fair Dealing" (2000) 116 LQR 66, 69. That the obligation has these three elements is consistent with Australian authority: *Alcatel Australia Ltd v Scarcella* (1998) 44 NSWLR 349, 369 (Sheller JA, with Powell and Beazley JJA agreeing), *Burger King Corpn v Hungry Jack's Pty Ltd* [2001] NSWCA 187; 69 NSWLR 558, para 171 (Sheller, Beazley and Stein JJA).
> 147. However, a contractual obligation of good faith does not require a party to act in the interests of the other party or to subordinate its own legitimate interest to the interests of the other party; although it does require it to have due regard to the legitimate interests of both parties: cf *Overlook v Foxtel* [2002] NSWSC 17 at [65]–[67] (Barrett J).
> 148. Applying that approach to the HOA, in my opinion the obligation of utmost good faith did not go so far as to require Area Health to defer to the interests of MHC and/or Macquarie in developing its own plans for [the hospital], or to include MHC and/or Macquarie in its own planning processes. But in my opinion, when Area Health's planning processes would make a substantial difference to what MHC and/or Macquarie could reasonably expect concerning the flow of persons between the hospitals or the creation of a campus concept, the obligation of utmost good faith would require that MHC and/or Macquarie be informed of this, at least to enable them to take account of it in the design and construction of the works contemplated by the HOA."

In *Astor Management AG v Atalaya Mining Plc* [2017] 2 B.C.L.C. 119, Leggatt J observed:

> "I have discussed elsewhere the question of whether or when there is in English law an implied duty to perform a contract in good faith: see *Yam Seng Pte Ltd v International Trade Corp Ltd* [2013] EWHC 111 (QB), [2013] 1 CLC 662. I do not think that this case is the occasion to explore that question further. A duty to act in good faith, where it exists, is a modest requirement. It does no more than reflect the expectation that a contracting party will act honestly towards the other party and will not conduct itself in a way which is calculated to frustrate the purpose of the contract or which would be regarded as commercially unacceptable by reasonable and honest people. This is a lesser duty than the positive obligation to use all reasonable endeavours to achieve a specified result which the contract in this case imposed."

In holding the "reasonable endeavours" obligation enforceable, the learned judge observed:

> "Far from being 'exceptional', I would say that it should almost always be possible to give sensible content to an undertaking to use reasonable endeavours (or 'all reasonable endeavours' or 'best endeavours') to enter into an agreement with a third party. There is no problem of uncertainty of object, as there is no inherent difficulty in telling whether an agreement with a third party has been made. Whether the party who gave the undertaking has endeavoured to make such an agreement (or used its best endeavours to do so) is a question of fact which a court can perfectly well decide. It may sometimes be hard to prove an absence of endeavours, or of best endeavours, but difficulty of proving a breach of a contractual obligation is an everyday occurrence and not a reason to hold that there is no obligation. Any complaint about lack of objective criteria could only be directed to the task of judging whether the endeavours used were 'reasonable', or whether there were other steps which it was reasonable to take so that it cannot be said that 'all reasonable endeavours' have been used. Where the parties have adopted a test of 'reasonableness', however, it seems to me that they are deliberately inviting the court to make a value judgment which sets a limit to their freedom of action.
>
> ...
>
> ... I do agree that a court will be very slow to second-guess a commercial party on matters of commercial judgment. For that reason, it may in many circumstances be extremely difficult or impossible to show that a party ought reasonably to have pursued a negotiation with a particular lender, or accepted a given offer, or proposed a lower rate of interest – to take the examples given by the defendants' counsel. But it is important to remember that the burden of proof is on the party alleging failure to comply with the obligation. Where the criticism involves a matter of fine judgment, it may be impossible to establish a breach. In other cases, however, the absence of reasonable endeavours may be obvious. It does not follow from the fact that there may often be difficulty in proof that there is no obligation at all or that the obligation has no sensible content."

A COLLATERAL SHAREHOLDERS' AGREEMENT

To the end of the paragraph, add:

3-59 In contrast to articles of association, there is no presumption in construing a shareholders' agreement in favour of freedom to transfer shares: *United Co Rusal Plc v Crispian Investments Ltd* [2018] EWHC 2415 (Comm)

ENTRENCHMENT OF RIGHTS OF INDIVIDUAL SHAREHOLDERS

To the end of the paragraph, add:

3-62 Section 22(2) of CA 2006 is not yet in force.

CHAPTER 4

Directors' Duties

TABLE OF CONTENTS

Principle 6—directors' duties	4-01
Companies Act 2006—Commencement and Transition	4-02
The New Statutory Code for Directors' Duties and its Relationship with Existing Law	4-03■
Relevance of Breach of Directors' Duties to the Statutory Oppression Remedies	4-21
Ratification of Directors' Breaches by the Members	4-23
Background: The Fiduciary Status of Directors	4-29■
The Duty of Good Faith	4-34
The Duty to Exercise Powers for a Proper Purpose	4-45
The Duty to Avoid Conflict of Interest and Duty	4-51
Section 175	4-57
Section 176	4-59
Section 177	4-61
The Leaving Director	4-63
Pre-2006 Act Principles	4-65■
Modification/dilution of the "No Conflict" Rule by the Articles of Association or shareholders' agreement	4-75■
The Relevance of a Conflict of Interest in the Application of the Other Directors' Duties	4-87■
The Leaving Director—Directorship Weakened or Terminated	4-92
Equitable Relief for Breach of the "No Conflict" Rule	4-100
The Duty to Exercise Independent Judgment	4-102
The Duty of Care	4-108
The Power to Issue Shares	4-115
Relief by the Court	4-130■
Transactions Between the Company and Directors Requiring Approval by the Members	4-131
Limitation	4-133■
Acquiescence and Laches	4-136

THE NEW STATUTORY CODE FOR DIRECTORS' DUTIES AND ITS RELATIONSHIP WITH EXISTING LAW

A duty owed to creditors?

To the end of the paragraph, add:
Re HLC Environmental Projects Ltd [2014] B.C.C. 337 was applied in *Hedger* **4-20**

v Adams [2016] B.C.C. 390 and *Ball v Hughes* [2018] B.C.C. 196. *BTI 2014 LLC v Sequana SA* [2017] 1 B.C.L.C. 453 was applied in *Dickinson v NAL Realisations (Staffordshire) Ltd* [2018] 1 B.C.L.C. 623, *Singularis Holdings Ltd (In Official Liquidation) v Daiwa Capital Markets Europe Ltd* [2017] 1 B.C.L.C. 625, and *LRH Services Ltd v Trew* [2018] EWHC 600 (Ch).

BACKGROUND: THE FIDUCIARY STATUS OF DIRECTORS

Replace third paragraph with:

4-31   The extent to which a director's, or indeed any other fiduciary's, duties in relation to conflicts of interest may in effect be modified or diluted, whether expressly or by necessary implication, and whether by direct modification or exclusion of the duty or acquiescence in or ratification of the breach thereof,[22] by the articles of association, or an agreement between shareholders, or as a necessary corollary of all the surrounding circumstances of their relationship and conduct, is a matter of some complexity and a highly fact-sensitive exercise: see paras 4-10–4-12 above, and paras 4-71, 4-75–4-83, 4-105, 4-130 and 11-69–11-76 below. This issue was revisited by the HKCFA in *Poon Ka Man Mason v Cheng Wai Tao* (2016) 19 HKCFAR 144. Reference may also be made to para.4-69: is the corporate opportunity in question one caught by the rule against conflict of interest and duty? See notes under that paragraph below. Just as the fully informed beneficiary has the power to dispense with or modify the duties owed to it by the fiduciary, so sometimes the beneficiary will have agreed to or acquiesced in the fiduciary having more than one master: see *Ultraframe (UK) Ltd v Fielding* [2006] F.S.R. 17, per Lewison J at [1312]–[1317].[23]

[22] But see the limits to the circumstances in which the majority may ratify a breach of director's duty: paras 5-36 et seq. below.

[23] See also *Movitex v Bulfield* [1988] B.C.L.C. 104 Ch D; *Edge v Pensions Ombudsman* [2000] Ch. 602 CA (Civ Div) at 632–633; *Hillsdown Holdings Plc v Pensions Ombudsman* [1997] 1 All E.R. 862 QBD. In *Murad v Al-Saraj* [2005] W.T.L.R. 1573, both Arden LJ and Jonathan Parker LJ questioned whether the rule against conflicts of interest was appropriate in the modern world and welcomed its review by the House of Lords (now the Supreme Court).

PRE-2006 ACT PRINCIPLES

The strictness of the "no conflict" rule

To the end of the paragraph, add:

4-69   See *Re Micra Contracts Ltd (In Liquidation)* [2016] B.C.C. 153, [19]–[22].

To the end of the paragraph, add:

4-69   The HKCFA doubted *Re Allied Business & Financial Consultants Ltd* [2009] B.C.C. 822 (CA), and its distinguishing of *Aas v Benham* as confined to partnership, in *Poon Ka Man Mason v Cheng Wai Tao* (2016) 19 HKCFAR 144—observing that "it would be surprising if a different rule applied to directors and partners—the latter being an equally well-established category of fiduciary relationship" [85]–[87]. However, by a majority, the court held that on the facts the director was accountable to the company as a fiduciary for businesses he had set up on his own behalf in competition with the company's.

Replace paragraph 4-71 with:

4-71   In a context which has in recent years proved especially difficult and controversial, namely that of a current or former director exploiting a corporate opportunity for his own benefit (see further paras 4-92 et seq. below for the case of the leaving director), a useful modern statement of the fundamental equitable principle, drawing attention to the fact-sensitive and flexible nature of the analysis required,[37] is to be found in the judgment of Jonathan Parker LJ in *Bhullar v Bhullar* [2003] B.C.C. 711:

> "[27] I agree ... that the concept of a conflict between fiduciary duty and personal interest presupposes an existing fiduciary duty. But it does not follow that it is a prerequisite of the accountability of a fiduciary that there should have been some improper dealing with property 'belonging' to the party to whom the fiduciary duty is owed, that is to say with trust property. The relevant rule, which Lord Cranworth LC in *Aberdeen Rly Co v Blaikie Bros* (1854) 1 Macq 461 at 471, [1843–60] All ER Rep 249 at 252 described as being 'of universal application', and which Lord Herschell in *Bray v Ford* [1895–99] All ER Rep 1009 at 1011, [1896] AC 44 at 51, described as 'inflexible', is that (to use Lord Cranworth's formulation) no fiduciary—
>
>> 'shall be allowed to enter into engagements in which he has, or can have, a personal interest conflicting, or which may possibly conflict, with the interests of those whom he is bound to protect.'
>
> [28] In a case such as the present, where a fiduciary has exploited a commercial opportunity for his own benefit, the relevant question, in my judgment, is not whether the party to whom the duty is owed (the company, in the instant case) had some kind of beneficial interest in the opportunity: in my judgment that would be too formalistic and restrictive an approach. Rather, the question is simply whether the fiduciary's exploitation of the opportunity is such as to attract the application of the rule. As Lord Upjohn made clear in *Boardman v Phipps* [1967] 2 A.C. 46 at 123, flexibility of application is of the essence of the rule. Thus, he said:
>
>> 'Rules of equity have to be applied to such a great diversity of circumstances that they can be stated only in the most general terms and applied with particular attention to the exact circumstances of each case.'
>
> Later in his speech Lord Upjohn gave this warning against attempting to reformulate the rule by reference to the facts of particular cases ([1967] 2 A.C. 46 at 125):
>
>> 'The whole of the law is laid down in the fundamental principle exemplified in Lord Cranworth's statement [in *Aberdeen Rly Co v Blaikie Brothers* (1854) 1 Macq 461] ... . But it is applicable, like so many equitable principles which may affect a conscience, however innocent, to such a diversity of different cases that the observations of judges and even in your lordships' House in cases where this great principle is being applied must be regarded as applicable only to the particular facts of the particular case in question and not regarded as a new and slightly different formulation of the legal principle so well settled.'
>
> [29] To my mind that warning is particularly apt in the instant case, given that the joint bundle of authorities which has been placed before us contains no less than 23 authorities, including Australian and American authorities.
>
> [30] As it seems to me, the rule is essentially a simple one, albeit that it may in some cases be difficult to apply. The only qualification which is required to Lord Cranworth's formulation of it is that which was supplied by Lord Upjohn in *Boardman v Phipps* [1967] 2 AC 46 at 124, where he said:
>
>> 'The phrase "possibly may conflict" requires consideration. In my view it means that the reasonable man looking at the relevant facts and circumstances of the particular case would think that there was a real sensible possibility of conflict; not that you could imagine some situation arising which might, in some conceivable possibility in events not contemplated as real sensible possibilities by any reasonable person, result in conflict.'[38]

[31] The strictness of the rule, and the flexibility of its application, was stressed by Lord Wilberforce in the Privy Council decision in *New Zealand Netherlands Society 'Oranje' Inc v Kuys*, [1973] 1 W.L.R. 1126 at 1129, where he said:

> 'The obligation not to profit from a position of trust, or, as it sometimes relevant to put it, not to allow a conflict to arise between duty and interest, is one of strictness. The strength, and indeed the severity, of the rule has recently been emphasised by the House of Lords in *Boardman v Phipps* ... It retains its vigour in all jurisdictions where the principles of equity are applied. Naturally it has different applications in different contexts. It applies, in principle, whether the case is one of a trust, express or implied, of partnership, of directorship of a limited company, of principal and agent, or master and servant, but the precise scope of it must be moulded according to the nature of the relationship.'"

See *Gamatronic (UK) Ltd v Hamilton* [2017] B.C.C. 670 for a recent decision on breach of duties by former directors and employees in setting up competing businesses. It was not sufficient that the defendants did not consider themselves to be competing—the position had to be determined objectively, citing *One Step (Support) Ltd v Morris-Garner* [2017] Q.B. 1.

[37] The general principles have been applied in a wide variety of circumstances, e.g. *Guinness v Saunders* [1990] 2 A.C. 663; *Neptune (Vehicle Washing Equipment) Ltd v Fitzgerald (No.2)* [1995] B.C.C. 1000 Ch D; *CMS Dolphin Ltd v Simonet* [2002] B.C.C. 600 Ch D; *Hunter v Kane* [2003] EWHC 186 (Ch) at [25]; *In Plus Group Ltd v Pyke* [2003] B.C.C. 332; *British Midland Tool Ltd v Midland International Tooling Ltd* [2003] 2 B.C.L.C. 523; *Crown Dilmun v Sutton* [2004] 1 B.C.L.C. 468; *Gwembe Valley Development v Koshy* [2004] 1 B.C.L.C. 131 at [44]–[45]; *Quarter Master UK Ltd (Inn Liquidation) v Pyke* [2005] 1 B.C.L.C. 245; *Fassihi v Item Software (UK) Ltd* [2004] B.C.C. 994; *Newgate Stud Co v Penfold* [2008] 1 B.C.L.C. 46; *Ultraframe v Fielding* [2006] F.S.R. 17; *Murad v Al-Saraj* [2005] W.T.L.R. 1573; *Wilkinson v West Coast Capital* [2007] B.C.C. 717; *Shepherds Investments Ltd v Walters* [2007] 2 B.C.L.C. 202; *Foster Bryant Surveying v Bryant* [2007] Bus. L.R. 1565; *Streeter v Western Areas Exploration (No.2)* [2011] WASCA 17; *Links Golf Tasmania v Sattler* [2012] F.C.A. 634; *Northampton Regional Livestock Centre Co Ltd v Cowling* [2016] 1 B.C.L.C. 431. The summary in *Hunter v Kane* [2002] EWHC 186 at [25] is helpful: *Northampton Regional Livestock Centre Co Ltd v Cowling* [2014] EWHC 30 (QB) at [196]–[197].

[38] This is reflected in the formulation of the duty to avoid conflicts of interest and the associated duties in ss.175–177. The duty arises where the director's interest "conflicts, or possibly may conflict, with the interests of the company" (s.175(1)), but is not infringed "if the situation cannot reasonably be regarded as likely to give rise to a conflict of interest" (s.175(4)(a). See the equivalent provisions in s.176(4) and s.177(6)(a).'

MODIFICATION/DILUTION OF THE "NO CONFLICT" RULE BY THE ARTICLES OF ASSOCIATION OR SHAREHOLDERS' AGREEMENT

Historical background

4-83
To the end of the paragraph, add:
See *Poon Ka Man Mason v Cheng Wai Tao* (2016) 19 HKCFAR 144, noted under para.4-69.

THE LEAVING DIRECTOR—DIRECTORSHIP WEAKENED OR TERMINATED

4-93
To the end of the paragraph, add:
See *Poon Ka Man Mason v Cheng Wai Tao* (2016) 19 HKCFAR 144, noted under para.4-69.

RELIEF BY THE COURT

To the end of the paragraph, add:
See *Cullen Investments Ltd v Brown* [2017] EWHC 2793 (Ch) and *LRH Services Ltd v Trew* [2018] EWHC 600 (Ch): in both cases, the court declined to grant relief from liability.

4-130

LIMITATION

To the end of the paragraph, add:
The application of s.21(1)(b) of the Limitation Act to misfeasant company directors has recently been settled by the Supreme Court in *Burnden Holdings (UK) Ltd v Fielding* [2018] 2 W.L.R. 885. The assumed facts were that the misappropriated assets had been received by companies in which the misfeasant director was a majority shareholder, not the director personally. In the Court of Appeal [2017] 1 W.L.R. 39, it had been held that this made no difference to the application of s.21(1)(b):

4-133

> "37. ... I consider that the judge was right in his construction of section 21(1)(b). The significance of control of a company is that it enables the controller to obtain, in a number of ways, the benefit of the assets of the company, or indeed the assets themselves or their proceeds of sale, provided that all statutory and other legal restrictions are observed. If section 21(1)(b) were construed to apply only to those cases where the trustee directly and personally acquires the trust property, its evident purpose would be much constrained and easily avoided. In my judgment, a construction which includes within its terms a transfer to a company directly or indirectly controlled by the trustee is within the meaning of this provision.
>
> 38. [Counsel for the director] also objected that an account of profits is not within section 21(1)(b). I am inclined to agree, but the remedies sought by the claimant include equitable compensation and that appears to me to be an appropriate remedy falling within section 21(1)(b), particularly where, as in the case of Mrs Fielding, the trustee's indirect interest in the trust asset has been converted to the use of the trustee.
>
> 39. It follows, in my judgment, that the claim in this action, so far as it relates to the indirect interests in the share in Vital received by the defendants, is one to which no limitation period applies by reason of section 21(1)(b)." (Per David Richards LJ.)

The Supreme Court, dismissing the appeal, held:

(i) it was clear beyond argument that directors of an English company are to be regarded by analogy as trustees within s.21, and the company was the beneficiary of the trust: [11];

(ii) the directors are to be treated as being in possession of the company property from the outset: [19]. So, in their case, the requirement that the property be previously received by them before its conversion is otiose;

(iii) it makes no difference that the misfeasant directors may not control the company as the majority on its board: [21];

(iv) s.21(1)(b) applied because the directors were the company's fiduciary stewards from the outset and the company's property had been misappropriated to the directors' own use because of the economic benefit which they stood to derive: [22]; and

(v) there was no challenge to the analysis in [38] of the Court of Appeal's judgment (above), i.e. the remedy of an account of profits was not, but an award of equitable compensation was, within s.21(1)(b): [13].

The issue is complicated where the misfeasant director's breach of duty does not involve a misapplication of company property. That issue was addressed in *First Subsea Ltd (formerly BSW Ltd) v Balltec Ltd* [2018] Ch. 25. In that case the company claimed an account of profits made by a director who had fraudulently set up a competing business in breach of his fiduciary duties owed to the company. It was held that s.21(1)(a) applied and that the defendant was not in that class of constructive trustees, as in *Williams v Central Bank of Nigeria*, who could rely upon a six-year limitation period. It was stated obiter that the *Gwembe Valley Development v Koshy* [2004] 1 B.C.L.C. 131 case, the authority for the proposition set out in (5) of para.4-134 and referenced in fn.66, was rightly decided: [57]. But this is subject to [38] of the judgment of David Richards LJ in *Burnden Holdings v Fielding*, where he observed that a claim for equitable compensation arising out of the conversion by a director of the company's asset to his use did come within s.21(1)(b), whereas a claim for an account of profits did not: see above.

To the end of the paragraph, add:

4-133   See also *Haysport Properties Ltd v Ackerman* [2016] B.C.C. 676 as to the circumstances in which it is proper to find that a director acted fraudulently for the purposes of s.21(1)(a) and s.32(1)(b) and (2) respectively.

Replace paragraph 4-134 with:

(1) Section 21 of the Limitation Act 1980 provides:

> "Time limit for actions in respect of trust property. (1) No period of limitation prescribed by this Act shall apply to an action by a beneficiary under a trust, being an action (a) in respect of any fraud or fraudulent breach of trust to which the trustee was a party or privy; or (b) to recover from the trustee trust property or the proceeds of trust property in the possession of the trustee, or previously received by the trustee and converted to his use ... (3) Subject to the preceding provisions of this section, an action by a beneficiary to recover trust property or in respect of any breach of trust, not being an action for which a period of limitation is prescribed by an other provision of this Act, shall not be brought after the expiration of six years from the date on which the right of action accrued ... ."

Section 32 of the Limitation Act 1980 further postpones the running of time for fraudulent concealment.

(2) So, the starting point is that a six-year limitation period will apply, applied either directly or by analogy. Personal claims against directors will normally be subject to limits by analogy with claims in tort or contract: see *Cia de Seguros Imperio v Heath (REBX) Ltd (formerly CE Heath & Co (America) Ltd)* [2001] 1 W.L.R. 112 CA (Civ Div).

(3) By virtue of the s.21(1)(a) exception, no period of limitation applies to fraud claims.

(4) By virtue of the s.21(1)(b) exception, no period of limitation applies to claims against a director as constructive trustee of company property which he has misappropriated to his own use.[65] The reason for this is that the director was in possession of the company property as a fiduciary for the company and continues to be accountable to the company for it notwithstanding any wrongful dealing on his part with it.

(5) However, s.21(1)(b) does not cover a claim against a director for an account of profits arising out of a breach of his duty.[66]

Section 32 of the Limitation Act 1980 postpones the running of time in the case of fraudulent concealment until the defrauded party has knowledge. For that purpose, there was much to be said for a simple rule that shareholder knowledge should not be attributed to the defrauded company: *Julien v Evolving TecKnologies & Enterprise Development Co Ltd* [2018] B.C.C. 376.

[65] *JJ Harrison v Harrison* [2002] B.C.C. 729. It has been held that s.21(1)(b) covers a case where a director misapplies the company's money so as to confer a benefit on a company under the director's control: *Burnden Holdings (UK) Ltd v Fielding* [2016] C.P. Rep. 41.

[66] *Gwembe Valley Development v Koshy* [2004] 1 B.C.L.C. 131. Applied in *JD Wetherspoon Plc v Van de Berg & Co Ltd* [2007] P.N.L.R. 28, on a striking out application, and [2009] 16 E.G. 138 (C.S.) at trial. But distinguished in *Burnden Holdings v Fielding*, where it was held that s.21(1)(b) may cover a claim for equitable compensation against a director.

CHAPTER 5

Majority Rule and Equitable Constraints

TABLE OF CONTENTS

Groups and Joint Ventures	5-01
Companies	5-08
Division of Roles Between Board of Directors and Shareholders	5-12
Principle 7—shareholders' control	5-12■
Court's Power to Call a General Meeting	5-26
Majority Rule	5-29
Principle 8—majority rule	5-30■
Principle 9—voting rights as property	5-30■
Ratification by Members of Breach of Duty by a Director	5-36
Equitable Constraints on Majority Rule	5-41■
Principle 13—equitable doctrine of "fraud on the minority"	5-41■

DIVISION OF ROLES BETWEEN BOARD OF DIRECTORS AND SHAREHOLDERS

PRINCIPLE 7—SHAREHOLDERS' CONTROL

Right to inspect the company's books and records

To the end of the paragraph, add:
   Sharp v Blank [2015] EWHC 3220 (Ch) is now reported at [2017] B.C.C. 187: see also notes under para.11-46. In that case, shareholders in Lloyds Bank sued former directors of the bank for breach of their fiduciary duties in relation to the bank's takeover of another bank, HBOS. It was common ground that the directors owed a duty to provide the shareholders with sufficient information to enable them to make an informed decision about how to vote in relation to the proposed acquisition. It was also common ground that this duty entailed a duty not to mislead or conceal material information and to advise shareholders in clear and comprehensible terms. Newey J held that the first task was to determine the content of that duty: [18]. He continued:

5-23

> "19 It seems to me therefore that rather than starting with whether the sufficient information duty is a fiduciary duty and arguing for its content from that, the correct starting point is to identify what the content of the sufficient information duty is. This can be found conveniently set out in the judgment of Neuberger J in *Re RAC Motoring Services Ltd* [2000] 1 B.C.L.C. 307, an earlier round of litigation arising out of the disposal by the RAC of its motoring services business. At 327a–c, he cites from the Australian decision of *Residues Treatment & Trading Co Ltd v Southern Resources Ltd* (1988) 14 A.C.L.R. 375

at 377–378 where White J said:

> 'The directors have a duty in equity to give to shareholders sufficient information for them to make informed decisions about proposals to be put them at meetings.'

And

> 'The essence of the duty is reasonableness or fairness in the circumstances having regard to the interests of the company as a whole.'

20 White J referred in that case to the duty being of long standing, and Neuberger J himself cites at 326a-i from two cases from the end of the 19th century, *Kaye v Croydon Tramways Co* [1898] 1 Ch. 358, and *Tiessen v Henderson* [1899] 1 Ch. 861. Both cases characterise the rule as a rule of ordinary fairness: in the former case Sir Nathaniel Lindley MR refers to 'ordinary fairness of language' and Rigby LJ to the purpose of the meeting being 'fairly and in language that could be understood by ordinary people disclosed'; and in the latter case Kekewich J refers to the shareholder having 'fair warning of what was to be submitted to the meeting'.

21 I do not find in these citations—or in anything else that I was shown—any suggestion that the sufficient information duty shares the characteristics typical of fiduciary duties owed by those who have undertaken to act in the interests of others and who have agreed to serve the interests of others with loyalty. The wellspring of this duty is not that the directors have agreed to put the interests of the shareholders first, but the much more simple one that if they are going to invite the shareholders to a meeting, common fairness requires that they explain what the purpose of the meeting is. That includes being clear and comprehensible and not misleading or tricky; but the reason for this is one of fairness, not of loyalty.

22 In these circumstances I am very doubtful if it is appropriate to describe this duty as a fiduciary duty at all, but whether or not that is so (and as I have already said [counsel for the defendants] accepted that this was arguable), it does not seem to me that the duty includes all the usual attributes of fiduciary duties as set out in Mothew's case."

See *Burberry Group Plc v Fox-Davies* [2017] B.C.C. 387 for an application of ss.116 et seq of the 2006 Act.

MAJORITY RULE

PRINCIPLE 9—VOTING RIGHTS AS PROPERTY

To the end of the paragraph, add:

5-31　See the discussion of the recognition of fiduciary duties in what may loosely be described as joint ventures in para.11-69 et seq.

In *Children's Investment Fund Foundation (UK) v Attorney General* [2018] Ch. 371, the court recognized the principle that a shareholder in a limited liability trading company, when voting for or against a resolution, was exercising a right of property to vote as he thought fit. But it held that this did not apply to an exclusively charitable company limited by guarantors, whose members stood by virtue of the provisions of the Charity Act 2011 in a fiduciary relation to the company.

EQUITABLE CONSTRAINTS ON MAJORITY RULE

PRINCIPLE 13—EQUITABLE DOCTRINE OF "FRAUD ON THE MINORITY"

Special resolution to alter the articles of association

To the end of the first paragraph, add:
 Re Charterhouse Capital [2015] B.C.C. 574 was followed by the Privy Council in *Staray Capital Ltd v Yang (aka Stanley)* [2017] UKPC 43, where the summary of the law by Sir Terence Etherton C (as he then was) at [90] was approved.

5-46

Generally

To the end of the paragraph, add:
 The recent case of *Staray Capital Ltd v Yang (aka Stanley)* [2017] UKPC 43 shows how difficult it is to persuade a court to find that a majority acted in bad faith in passing a special resolution to change the articles even so as to give itself the power to expropriate a minority shareholder. The case was bizarre. The 80% majority shareholder fell out with the 20% minority shareholder, the former alleging that he had been misled into agreeing to go into the joint venture with the latter and that the company had been damaged by the actions of the latter. So he removed the minority as a director and passed a special resolution so as to add an article which enabled the company acting by its board (i.e. the majority shareholder) to require the buy-out of any shareholder at a fair value who had made material misrepresentations when acquiring his shares or whose actions had resulted in detriment to the company. Having passed that special resolution, the company then issued a redemption notice to purchase the minority's shares. The minority shareholder brought unfair prejudice proceedings, not to be bought out at a valuation conducted by the court, but to strike down the compulsory expropriation procedure and to stop any further issue of shares: as Bannister J observed at the beginning of his judgment at first instance, the proceedings were brought to "fossilize ... the affairs of the company for the foreseeable (and indeed for the unforeseeable) future". He observed that this was a category (i) case as analysed by Lord Hoffmann in *Citco Banking Corp NV v Pusser's Ltd* [2007] Bus L.R. 960 (i.e. the interests of the company, as opposed to the shareholders, were engaged) and held that, regardless of whether or not the change in the articles was valid, the redemption notice was invalid because the minority had not made any material misrepresentations or acted in a manner detrimental to the company. So, the minority shareholder substantially succeeded. Nevertheless, he declined to find that the majority had acted in bad faith in passing the special resolution to add that article and he held that the resolution was validly passed. All his findings were upheld on appeal: in relation to the latter finding, as the Privy Council put it at [38], it was the subjective view of the majority shareholder, whether or not mistaken, which was "determinative, unless it was a view which no reasonable person could have held".

5-50

CHAPTER 6

The Derivative Claim

TABLE OF CONTENTS

Principle 10—The proper claimant	6-01
Principle 12—exception to the proper claimant principle: the derivative claim	6-02
Companies Act 2006—The New Statutory Regime	6-03■
The Rule in Foss v Harbottle and the "Fraud on the Minority" Exception Thereto	6-10■
The New Statutory Regime: Part 11 of the 2006 Act	6-23■
The Grant or Refusal by the Court of Permission to Continue the Derivative Claim	6-37■
Threshold Criteria	6-44■
Factors Going to Exercise of Discretion	6-51■
The Powers of the Court	6-70
Application to Take Over Proceedings as Derivative Proceedings	6-73
The "Double-Derivative" Claim	6-74■
Procedure	6-77■
Principle 12 (continued)	6-77■
Wallersteiner and Other Costs Orders	6-89
Participation by the Company	6-103
Personal Rights	6-108
The Unfair Prejudice Remedy	6-111
Arbitration Clauses	6-114
Foreign Companies	6-115

COMPANIES ACT 2006—THE NEW STATUTORY REGIME

Replace paragraph 6-08 with:

A derivative claim which falls within the statutory definition of such a claim in s. 260(1) can now *only* be brought if sanctioned by the court under the new code or ss.994–6 of the 2006 Act.[10] It is not, however, an exhaustive code. Derivative claims which do not fall within that definition, such as "double-derivative" claims (see para.6-74 below) and claims in respect of wrongs done to foreign companies and other business vehicles not covered by the Act (see para.12-08 below), may still be brought outside the statutory code: *Re Fort Gilkicker Ltd* [2013] Ch. 551; *Abouraya v Sigmund* [2015] B.C.C. 503. In this respect, the old law relating to the exceptions to the rule in *Foss v Harbottle* remain of direct relevance. See *Harris v Microfusion 2003-2 LLP* [2017] 1 B.C.L.C. 305, noted under para.6-20.

6-08

---

[10] See per Lewison J in *Iesini v Westrip Holdings Ltd* [2010] B.C.C. 420 at [81]–[82].

THE RULE IN FOSS V HARBOTTLE AND THE "FRAUD ON THE MINORITY" EXCEPTION THERETO

To the end of the paragraph, add:

6-14   A beneficial owner of shares, claiming conversion of the shares, can bring derivative proceedings if the trustees refuse to sue but had no standing to bring a claim in his personal capacity: *McEneaney v Stevens* unreported, 2 May 2017 (Ch D)

To the end of the paragraph, add:

6-20   In *Harris v Microfusion 2003-2 LLP* [2017] 1 B.C.L.C. 305, it was common ground that the new statutory derivative remedy did not apply to limited liability partnerships and that the common law derivative remedy had survived the enactment of the statutory remedy: see the decision of Briggs J (as he then was) in *Re Fort Gilkicker Ltd* [2013] Ch. 551. It was argued by the claimant, in reliance upon *Estmanco (Kilner House) Ltd v Greater London Council* [1982] 1 W.L.R. 2, that it was not a requirement of the "fraud on minority" exception, in the absence of fraud, that the defendant directors had themselves benefitted from their alleged wrongdoing. The court rejected this argument and approved the summaries of the law in the citations in paras 6-19 and 6-20, from *Daniels v Daniels* and *Abouraya v Sigmund*:

> "29 I think that it is clear that *Estmanco* was a case where the majority was seeking to use the alleged breach of duty to further its own ends and in that sense to gain a personal benefit, albeit political rather than financial, and therefore was (allegedly) using its majority voting power to commit a 'fraud on the minority'. To that extent it is on all fours with *Daniels v Daniels*.
>
> ...
>
> 33 ... Essentially, people are free to join as members of corporate entities upon whatever terms they choose, formulated in articles of association, partnership deeds for LLPs or shareholders' agreements. They are bound by such arrangements and if majority rule is provided for, the minority is bound by the wishes of the majority. The majority can choose to excuse breaches of duty by directors, provided that the majority have not used their voting powers to confer benefits upon themselves in breach of duty and are not using the self-same powers to prevent the company from recovering the loss caused to it, in effect expropriating the minority in the process. The constraints imposed by equity make an exception to the rule in *Foss v Harbottle* in cases where the controlling members are precluded from ratifying the relevant breach by exercise of their majority votes. Thus, the 'fraud on the minority' exception prevents directors from improperly benefitting themselves at the expense of the company." (Per McCombe LJ.)

In fn.20 to para.6-19, reference is made to the full review of the relevant authorities in relation to the rule in *Foss v Harbottle* in this context in the fifth edition of this work, at paras 6-15–6-18. The argument advanced and rejected in *Harris v Microfusion 2003-2 LLP* is essentially the analysis at para.6-18 of the fifth edition, which must now be taken to be incorrect, at least under English law short of the Supreme Court.

The above requirement in a common law derivative action, namely that either the cause of action be fraud or the allegedly wrongdoing directors benefited from their wrongdoing, does not apply to a statutory derivative claim.

Replace paragraph 6-022 with:

6-22   Thus, relevant factors include in particular (a) the nature of the cause of action that was alleged to lie by and on behalf of the company against the shareholder or director in question and (b) the degree of control exercised by the wrongdoers themselves over the company. Ultimately, the question which has to be answered

THRESHOLD CRITERIA

in order to determine whether the case falls within the "fraud on the minority" exception to the rule in *Foss v Harbottle* is: "Is a claim for the benefit of the company being improperly stifled?", see para.6-36 below. This involves consideration of all the circumstances, including the merits of the claim and the availability of alternative remedies.[22] In the light of *Harris v Microfusion 2003-2 LLP* [2017] 1 B.C.L.C. 305, noted under para.6-20, this is an oversimplification. In *Tremendous Success Holdings Ltd v Sinosoft Technology Group Ltd* [2016] HKEC 1509, the court refused to allow a common law derivative claim to proceed, on the basis that it was being pursued mala fides and for purposes other than benefiting the company.

[22] *Henderson PFI Secondary Fund II LLP v Henderson PFI Secondary Fund II LP* [2013] Q.B. 934.

THE NEW STATUTORY REGIME: PART 11 OF THE 2006 ACT

The cause of action that may be pursued as a derivative claim

To the end of the paragraph, add:
   The requirement in a common law derivative action (see *Harris v Microfusion 2003-2 LLP* [2017] 1 B.C.L.C. 305, noted under para.6-20), that either the cause of action be fraud or the allegedly wrongdoing directors benefited from their wrongdoing, does not apply to a statutory derivative claim.

6-23

To the end of the paragraph, add:
   In *SDI Retail Services Ltd v King* [2017] EWHC 737 (Ch) at [49], it was held that the derivative claim against a third party did not arise independently of the directors' breach of duty and therefore could be brought under the statutory regime.

6-26

Wrongdoer control

To the end of the paragraph, add:
   But see now *Harris v Microfusion 2003-2 LLP* [2017] 1 B.C.L.C. 305, noted under para.6-20.

6-36

THE GRANT OR REFUSAL BY THE COURT OF PERMISSION TO CONTINUE THE DERIVATIVE CLAIM

The nature and purpose of the inter partes permission hearing

To the end of the paragraph, add:
   As was observed in *SDI Retail Services Ltd v King* [2017] EWHC 737 (Ch) at [64], following *Stainer v Lee* [2011] B.C.C. 134 at [29], there is no particular standard of proof to be satisfied when applying the discretionary factors and the evaluation is not a mechanistic one: it may be in the interests of the company to pursue a weaker case for a larger sum, or a very strong case for a smaller sum.

6-43

THRESHOLD CRITERIA

(1) The duty to promote the success of the company

To the end of the paragraph, add:
   In *Zavahir v Shankleman* [2017] B.C.C. 500, permission was refused because,

6-48

taking into outcome the best outcome and the costs of the litigation, no prudent director carrying out a normal risk/benefit analysis would have sought to continue the claim.

FACTORS GOING TO EXERCISE OF DISCRETION

6-51
To the end of the paragraph, add:
As was observed in *SDI Retail Services Ltd v King* [2017] EWHC 737 (Ch) at [64], following *Stainer v Lee* [2011] B.C.C. 134 at [29], there is no particular standard of proof to be satisfied when applying the discretionary factors and the evaluation is not a mechanistic one. In *Goodwin v Cook* unreported, 25 June 2018 (Ch D) permission to bring a derivative claim was refused applying the discretionary factors and having regard to alternative remedies.

Whether the claimant has another remedy in his own right: s.263(3)(f)

6-59
To the end of the paragraph, add:
In *SDI Retail Services Ltd v King* [2017] EWHC 737 (Ch) at [82], it was held that any claim by the claimant in its own right for breach of contract would have fallen foul of the rule against reflective loss, and a s. 994 petition would not have been preferable since the claim sought to vindicate the company's rights

6-61
To the end of the paragraph, add:
In *Zavahir v Shankleman* [2017] B.C.C. 500, permission was refused on the alternative ground that the claimant had an alternative remedy in unfair prejudice

THE "DOUBLE-DERIVATIVE" CLAIM

6-74
To the end of the paragraph, add:
See *Harris v Microfusion 2003-2 LLP* [2017] 1 B.C.L.C. 305, noted under para.6-20.

PROCEDURE

PRINCIPLE 12 (CONTINUED)

6-78
To the end of the paragraph, add:
The court has jurisdiction to grant permission retrospectively: *Wilton UK Ltd v Shuttleworth* [2018] Bus. L.R. 258; [2018] EWHC 911 (Ch).

CHAPTER 7

The Unfair Prejudice Remedy: Principles

TABLE OF CONTENTS

Principle 14—the unfair prejudice remedy	7-01
Principle 16—equitable principles	7-02
The Statutory Concept of Unfairness	7-05■
The Elements of Unfair Prejudice	7-41■
Breach of Agreements and Understandings (Including of Good Faith) Between Shareholders	7-80■
Other Equitable Principles	7-116
Breakdown of Trust and Confidence	7-117■
Breach of Fiduciary and Other Duties by Directors	7-122■
Relationship with the Derivative Claim	7-129■
Grounds for Winding-up on the Just and Equitable Basis	7-135■
Applications of the Unfair Prejudice Test	7-137■
Exit Routes Under Articles of Association and Shareholders' Agreements	7-189■
Arbitration Clauses	7-198■
"Clean Hands" and Misconduct on the Part of the Petitioner	7-200■
Delay and Acquiescence	7-205■
Collateral Purpose of Petitioner	7-211

THE STATUTORY CONCEPT OF UNFAIRNESS

O'Neill v Phillips

The legal analysis in the House of Lords

Replace "7-84" with:
7-85 **7-32**

A wider interpretation

After item "(4)", add:

(5) Why is the general right of a partner to management participation an equitable principle which is imported from the law of partnership by the statutory remedies for the protection of minority shareholders, whereas the equitable principles which flow from the fiduciary relationship between partners are not? See further para.7-104.

To the end of the paragraph, add:
There is little sign in recent English cases of any questioning of the emphasis placed by Lord Hoffmann in *O'Neill v Phillips* upon the applicability of **7-37**

"traditional" and "tolerably well settled" equitable principles, nor of any enthusiasm for the dicta of Arden LJ in *Re Tobian Properties*. See for example, *VB Football Assets v Blackpool Football Club (Properties) Ltd* [2017] EWHC 2767 (Ch), noted under para.7-94. The room for a broader interpretation of the concept of unfairness under English law probably lies in the recognition of circumstances where it is said (and so held in *Ebrahimi v Westbourne Galleries Ltd* [1973] A.C. 360) that the more elastic equitable principles of good faith derived from the law of partnership are held to apply, i.e. in "quasi-partnerships": see paras 7-89–7-115. If that is correct, then as was observed in *Re CY Foundation Group Ltd* [2013] HKEC 1209 at [81], [90]–[91], there may well be no difference between the approaches in the several common law jurisdictions with similarly worded oppression remedies. For a similar approach in Singapore, see *Lim Kok Wah v Lim Boh Yong* [2015] SGHC 211 at [99]–[121]; contrast *Over & Over Ltd v Bonvests Holdings Ltd* [2010] SGCA 7 (Singapore CA), where *O'Neill v Phillips* is not referred to in the judgment.

To the end of the paragraph, add:

7-40   For the approach in Singapore, see *Lim Kok Wah v Lim Boh Yong* [2015] SGHC 211 at [99]–[121]; contrast *Over & Over Ltd v Bonvests Holdings Ltd* [2010] SGCA 7 (Singapore CA).

THE ELEMENTS OF UNFAIR PREJUDICE

Element (1): Conduct of the affairs of the company

An act or omission of the company or the conduct of the company's affairs

Replace paragraph 7-52 with:

7-52   But, as the Court of Appeal in *Re Coroin* [2012] EWHC 521 (Ch) (David Richards J, interlocutory ruling); [2012] EWHC 2343 (Ch) (Richards J, trial); [2014] B.C.C. 14 at [168], emphasised, it is necessary to distinguish between the conduct by shareholders of their own affairs and the conduct of the affairs of the company. The trial judge, David Richards J (as he then was), provided the following summary[42]:

> "*The company's affairs*
>
> 626.   The purpose of the jurisdiction is to provide remedies in respect of the way in which the affairs of the company are conducted. It was perceived prior to the enactment of section 75 of the Companies Act 1980 that there was insufficient protection to shareholders in that respect. The section is not directed to the activities of shareholders amongst themselves, unless those activities translate into acts or omissions of the company or the conduct of its affairs. Relations between shareholders inter se are adequately governed by the law of contract and tort, including where appropriate the ability to enforce personal rights conferred by a company's articles of association. This important distinction has been emphasised in many of the authorities. In *Re Legal Negotiators Limited* [1999] BCC 547 the Court of Appeal upheld the decision of Peter Goldsmith QC, sitting as a deputy Judge of the Chancery Division, to strike out a petition under section 459 of the Companies Act 1985 as unsustainable. Peter Gibson LJ at page 550 summarised the judgment below, with which he said he completely agreed. He said that the Judge
>
>> 'reviewed the authorities from which he drew two points of significance for the case before him. The first was that the starting point was to consider what the parties had agreed between themselves as their commercial relationships, though he recognised this not need always be contained in the articles of association. The

second was that the essence of the powers under s.459 is to give a remedy where there is complaint about the way the company's affairs are being conducted through the use (or failure to use) powers in relation to the conduct of the company's affairs provided by its constitution. He regarded the section as concerned with the company's affairs rather than the affairs of individuals and to be concerned with acts done by the company or those authorised to act as its organs.'

At page 551, Peter Gibson L.J. said:

'Thus, like the Judge I too would lay emphasis on the need to show that it is the affairs of the company which are being or have been conducted in an unfairly prejudicial manner or that it is an act or omission of the company that is or would be so prejudicial. The conduct of a member of his own affairs, for example by requesting a general meeting of the company or seeking answers to an excessive number of questions, is irrelevant.'

I would only add that the refusal by a company to convene a general meeting would be an act of the company, although whether it was either unfair or prejudicial would of course depend on the circumstances. Other authorities in which the same distinction had been drawn include *In re Unisoft Group Limited (No. 2)* [1994] BCC 766, *In re Estate Acquisition and Development Limited* [1995] BCC 338 and *In re Leeds United Holdings Limited* [1997] BCC 131.

...

628. The Court will not adopt a technical or legalistic approach to what constitutes the affairs of the company but will look at the business realities. It was held by the Court of Appeal in *Rackind v Gross* [2005] 1 WLR 3505 that the affairs of a company could include the affairs of a wholly-owned subsidiary which had common directors. If the affairs of the subsidiary are being conducted in a manner which damages the subsidiary and hence the value of the holding company's interest in the subsidiary, then the omission of the directors of the holding company to take steps to rectify the situation seems to me plainly capable of falling within section 994(1). Likewise, where the directors of a partly owned subsidiary nominated by the holding company permitted the holding company to build up a business at the expense of the subsidiary's business, which was allowed to wither, without taking any steps to protect the subsidiary's position, they were engaged in the conduct of the affairs of the subsidiary: *Scottish Co-operative Wholesale Society Limited v Mayor* [1959] AC 324. See also the decision of Court of Session (Outer House) in *Whillock v Henderson* [2009] BCC 314.

629. By way of conclusion on this aspect, guidance was given by the Court of Appeal in *In re Neath Rugby Ltd (No.2)* [2009] 2 BCLC 427 where at para.50 of a judgment with which the other members of the Court agreed, Stanley Burnton LJ said:

'The judge cited the observations of Powell J in *Re Dernacourt Investments Pty Ltd* (1990) 2 ACSR 553: The words "affairs of a company" are extremely wide and should be construed liberally: (a) in determining the ambit of the "affairs" of a parent company for the purposes of s 320, the court looks at the business realities of a situation and does not confine them to a narrow legalistic view; (b) "affairs" of a company encompass all matters which may come before its board for consideration; (c) conduct of the "affairs" of a parent company includes refraining from procuring a subsidiary to do something or condoning by inaction an act of a subsidiary, particularly when the directors of the parent and the subsidiary are the same ... .

I would accept these propositions, but with some qualification. (b) may extend to matters which are capable of coming before the board for its consideration, and may not be limited to those that actually come before the board: I do not accept that matters that are not considered by the board are not capable of being part of its affairs. Nonetheless, like the judge, I am unable to see how it can be said that the affairs of Neath and of Osprey were so intermingled that all of the affairs of the latter were the affairs of the former. It would, for example, be quite irrational to suggest that Mr Blyth, when acting as a director of Osprey, was conducting the affairs of Neath.'

It no doubt goes without saying that the affairs of the company will also encompass matters which must go to the company in general meeting, rather than the board, for consideration."

In *Li Guozhu v New Century Iatrical Inv Management Ltd* [2018] HKEC 1021, it was held, following *Graham v Every* [2015] 1 B.C.L.C. 41, that a concerted attempt to defeat the petitioner's pre-emption rights in the context of a battle for control of the company was conduct of the company's affairs.

[42] See also per Arden LJ in *Graham v Every* [2014] B.C.C. 376 at [37]–[40]; and *Re Charterhouse Capital Ltd* [2015] B.C.C. 574 at [45]–[46].

Element (2): Interests as a shareholder

To the end of the paragraph, add:

7-66 See *Re Edwardian Group Ltd* [2018] EWHC 1715 (Ch), at [623].

To the end of the paragraph, add:

7-67 Agreements and understandings in quasi-partnerships, enforceable in equity as between the original shareholders, will not necessarily survive the transmission of the shares, such as transmission to subsequent generations in family companies.[53] See para.7-100; *Re Edwardian Group Ltd* [2018] EWHC 1715 (Ch), at [135]–[136]. In *Re Edwardian Group Ltd* [2018] EWHC 1715 (Ch), Fancourt J held obiter that a shareholder who was not party to or bound by an informal agreement or understanding enforceable in equity could not rely upon a breach thereof because there was no unfairness in the manner in which its interests had been prejudiced: [228].

[53] See *Murray's Judicial Factor* [1992] B.C.C. 596 CSIH; *Fisher v Cadman* [2006] 1 B.C.L.C. 499. See also the *Saul D Harrison* [1995] 1 B.C.L.C. 14 case at 19h.

Element (3): Prejudice

To the end of the paragraph, add:

7-74 See *Re OS3 Distribution Ltd* [2017] EWHC 2621 (Ch), where a procedural irregularity in convening a meeting was held not to have caused prejudice because it did not affect the outcome.

To the end of the paragraph, add:

7-75 See *Re Edwardian Group Ltd* [2018] EWHC 1715 (Ch), where it was held that a breach of fiduciary duty by the directors, such as not to place themselves in a position of conflict of personal interest and duty, or a biased investigation, could amount to unfair prejudice because it was "corrosive of good administration and trust between shareholders and directors": [339], [493], [606], [620].

BREACH OF AGREEMENTS AND UNDERSTANDINGS (INCLUDING OF GOOD FAITH) BETWEEN SHAREHOLDERS

(1) Breach of contract (including the articles of association)

Incomplete agreement

Replace second paragraph with:

7-85 And see per Jonathan Parker J in *Re Guidezone Ltd* [2001] B.C.C. 692 Ch D

(Comp) at [175], cited in para.7-99 below, as to the relevance of general equitable principles of estoppel: see also paras 11-61 et seq. As it was put in *Khoshkhou v Cooper* [2014] EWHC 1087 (Ch) at [24]:

> "[I]n principle such an agreement [i.e. breach of which would give rise to a claim of unfair prejudice] might be made at the time of or after he became a member, and need not be an agreement that would be separately enforceable as a matter of law. Thus, for instance, it would not necessarily be a bar to the equitable jurisdiction if the agreement made lacked the certainty to be enforceable as a contract. But in my judgment this does not mean that any assurance however vague can be treated as sufficient; the members must have reached a sufficient degree of agreement that it can be said that there has been a breach of good faith in departing from it."

See also para.7-111. See *VB Football Assets v Blackpool Football Club (Properties) Ltd* [2017] EWHC 2767 (Ch), noted under para.7-94, and *Generator Developments Ltd v Lidl UK GmbH* [2018] EWCA Civ 396, noted under para.11-60.

Change title of paragraph following paragraph 7-88 to:

(2) Rights, expectations and obligations between the members enforceable in equity, i.e. a "quasi-partnership" case

Existence of "quasi-partnership"

To the end of the paragraph, add:
In *Cha v Staray Capital Ltd* unreported 13 February 2013 (BVI), Bannister J, noted further under para.5-50 above, it was held that the mere fact that the 80% shareholder referred to the 20% shareholder as his "partner" did not make the joint venture a quasi-partnership: [14]–[19].

7-92

To the end of the paragraph, add:
In *VB Football Assets v Blackpool Football Club (Properties) Ltd* [2017] EWHC 2767 (Ch), the parties had entered into complex agreements but, because to do so would have adverse tax consequences, had decided not to reduce one aspect of the proposed deal to a binding agreement, namely that the minority shareholder would in due course acquire parity of shareholding and would have a joint say in its operation in the meantime. Marcus Smith J held that this understanding was considered by the parties to be "a gentleman's agreement unenforceable in law": [92]–[93], [321]. Having cited the passage from the speech of Lord Hoffmann in *O'Neill v Phillips* in which he had said that the court should stick to "tolerably well settled" equitable principles and not embrace "some wholly indefinite notion of fairness", the learned judge then observed that in the case before him there was "space for equitable considerations *or legitimate expectations*" (emphasis added) and went on to hold (at [322], [380]–[387]) that the above understanding gave rise to a legitimate expectation enforceable under the unfair prejudice remedy and precluded a minority discount in the valuation of the shares to be purchased. The use by the learned judge of the expression "legitimate expectation" is perhaps questionable. It appears that his attention was not drawn to the other passage in Lord Hoffmann's speech, cited in para.7-18, where Lord Hoffmann had rejected the use of the concept of "legitimate expectation" as subverting the relative certainty of equitable principles, reinforced in subsequent cases such as *Re Guidezone* [2014] 1 W.L.R. 3728, cited in para.7-99. But the outcome can perhaps be supported as in effect a finding that, notwithstanding the complex written agreements, the company was nevertheless an *Ebrahimi v Westbourne Galleries Ltd* [1973] A.C. 360 quasi-partnership, i.e a relationship based on trust and confidence where equitable du-

7-94

ties of good faith, derived from the law of partnership and imported by the statutory remedy, applied. It seems the learned Judge was not referred to authorities dealing with equitable principles in contexts other than the unfair prejudice remedy, which suggest that, outside the unfair prejudice remedy, breach of a "gentleman's agreement" may not give rise to equitable remedies: see para 11-58 et seq. and the recent decision of the Court of Appeal in *Generator Developments Ltd v Lidl UK GmbH* [2018] EWCA Civ 396.

Contrast *Re Edwardian Group Ltd* [2018] EWHC 1715 (Ch), at [213].

In *Lim Kok Wah v Lim Boh Yong* [2015] SGHC 211 at [99]–[121], it was held that there had to be "an informal agreement or a clear understanding" of management participation in order to ground relief under the Singaporean oppression remedy.

To the end of the paragraph, add:

7-96 In *Wootliff v Rushton-Turner (No.2)* [2018] 1 B.C.L.C. 479, it was held on the facts that the relationship between the parties was a purely commercial one, as opposed to one based on trust and confidence, which did not contain any basis for superimposing equitable duties against removal from office as a director.

In *Pinfold v Ansell* [2017] 2 B.C.L.C. 489 it was held that the relationship went beyond a master/servant relationship and amounted to a quasi-partnership.

To the end of the paragraph, add:

7-99 As Fancourt J put it in *Re Edwardian Group Ltd* [2018] EWHC 1715 (Ch):

"... [T]here must be something in the nature of the 'special underlying obligation' or the circumstances in which it arises that makes it enforceable in equity at the suit of the petitioner. An unenforceable agreement or understanding will not suffice: there must be something that makes it unconscionable for those controlling the company to disregard the agreement or understanding, and that will generally be found where there is mutuality between the shareholders as to the benefit and burden of the obligation, or some detrimental reliance or change of position that makes it inequitable to deny the obligation."
([127].)

He further held obiter that, because of the need for mutuality, it was difficult to envisage a company being a quasi-partnership where some but not all the shareholders were alleged to be bound by the "special underlying obligation":

"134. ... The quasi-partnership status of a company arises not just from an informal understanding arising between some or all shareholders (which would otherwise be unenforceable as a matter of contract) but from the particular character that the company has where there is a mutual relationship of trust and confidence, akin to a partnership, and where the agreement or understanding affects the conscience of the members of the company:

'Equitable considerations, affecting the manner in which legal rights can be exercised, will arise only in those cases where there exist considerations of a personal character between the shareholders which makes it unjust or inequitable to insist on legal rights or to exercise them in a particular way. (per David Richards J in *Re Coroin Ltd (No.2)* [2012] EWHC 2343 (Ch); [2013] 2 BCLC 583 at para [635])'

135. The understanding is enforceable in equity because of its mutuality: the mutual relationship of trust and confidence, of a personal character, affects the conscience of each member equally. Almost by definition, if the majority (by voting rights) of the members are not bound by any such mutual rights or understanding, the company does not have the characteristics of a partnership."

And see also [213] for the distinction he drew between an obligation enforceable in equity and an obligation lacking mutuality which was binding in honour only.

BREACH OF AGREEMENTS AND UNDERSTANDINGS 29

To the end of the paragraph, add:
See *Re Edwardian Group Ltd* [2018] EWHC 1715 (Ch) at [135]–[136] on the effect of a transmission of shares on a quasi-partnership. **7-100**

Partnership law—good faith in general

To the end of the paragraph, add:
Although it may be a general principle of partnership law that partners stand in a fiduciary relationship to one another, it is clear that shareholders, even if the relationship may be labeled one of "quasi-partnership", do not stand in a fiduciary relationship with one another save in the exceptional circumstances where such a relationship has been assumed: see Principle 9 and paras 5-31–5-35, and 11-69–11-78. So, the question arises: why is the general right of a partner to management participation an equitable principle which is imported from the law of partnership by the statutory remedies for the protection of minority shareholders, whereas the equitable principles which flow from the fiduciary relationship between partners are not? For this purpose, it is not enough to say that a company is not a partnership. **7-104**

Existence of duty of good faith

Replace paragraph 7-106 with:
In *Crawley v Short* (2009) 76 A.C.S.R. 286 at [113], the *Oak Investment Partners XII v Boughtwood* case (above) was treated by the New South Wales Court of Appeal as authority for the proposition that "[e]specially in a closely held corporation there will even be a duty on a non director not to act unconscionably to his or her fellow shareholders". In that case the court also held at [108]: **7-106**

> "… If the Court considers that the corporate entity is sufficiently closely held to be akin to a partnership it may consider that it is appropriate to hold that the directors have the same obligations to their co-members as a partner would have had … ."[75]

But *Crawley v Short* (2009) 76 A.C.S.R. 286 was analysed by Newey J in *Sharp v Blank* [2017] B.C.C. 187 at [10(5)] as a case where there was a special relationship between the directors and shareholders in question arising out of a purchase of the shares of one of three shareholders such that the former owed *fiduciary* duties to the latter: see the notes under para.11-46.

[75] See further, paras 11-69 et seq. below.

Breach of duty of good faith

To the end of the paragraph, add:
See para.3-26. **7-108**

Content of specific expectations and understandings

Replace second paragraph with:
In contrast to the facts in *O'Neill v Phillips*, where one party had refused to sign a formal agreement, the shareholders had proceeded and acted to their detriment on the basis that they were bound in good faith without the need for a formal signed agreement.[78] See *VB Football Assets v Blackpool Football Club (Properties) Ltd* [2017] EWHC 2767 (Ch) noted under para.7-94 above. **7-113**

[78] See the passage in the judgment of Jonathan Parker J in *Re Guidezone* [2000] 2 B.C.L.C. 321, cited in para.7-99 above.

BREAKDOWN OF TRUST AND CONFIDENCE

To the end of the paragraph, add:

7-117 In *Badyal v Badyal* [2018] EWHC 68 (Ch) it was reaffirmed that a mere breakdown in trust and confidence cannot of itself amount to either unfair prejudice or grounds for winding up on the just and equitable basis: [113]–[119].

BREACH OF FIDUCIARY AND OTHER DUTIES BY DIRECTORS

To the end of the paragraph, add:

7-127 In *Re Edwardian Group Ltd* [2018] EWHC 1715 (Ch), it was held that a breach of fiduciary duty by the directors, such as not to place themselves in a position of conflict of personal interest and duty, or a biased investigation, could amount to unfair prejudice merely because it was "corrosive of good administration and trust between shareholders and directors": [339], [493], [606], [620].

RELATIONSHIP WITH THE DERIVATIVE CLAIM

To the end of the paragraph, add:

7-129 See para.6-60 et seq. as to the discretion of the court to refuse permission to bring a derivative claim on the ground that the claimant has an alternative remedy, such as an unfair prejudice petition.

GROUNDS FOR WINDING-UP ON THE JUST AND EQUITABLE BASIS

To the end of the paragraph, add:

7-136 In *Badyal v Badyal* [2018] EWHC 68 (Ch) it appears to have been assumed that there was no difference between the two remedies.

APPLICATIONS OF THE UNFAIR PREJUDICE TEST

Exclusion from management

Replace first paragraph with:

7-138 It is clear[93] that in the case of a quasi-partnership it may be part of the real bargain between shareholders that a member is entitled to be involved in the management of a company, and in particular to be employed with a salary. Repudiation of that bargain by the exclusion of the minority by the majority will found a claim for unfair prejudice. For the difficulty in drawing the line between exclusion and voluntary departure, see para.7-121.

[93] Under s.210 of the Companies Act 1948, before the House of Lords decision in *Re Westbourne Galleries*, it was held that exclusion from management in a quasi-partnership did not found a petition under that section. In the early days of the unfair prejudice remedy, it was still a matter of argument whether, in the case of a quasi-partnership where the quasi-partners were entitled as a matter of good faith to participate in management, in other words the type of company considered *Re Westbourne Galleries*, a member could complain about exclusion from management: see *Re Company (No.002567 of 1982)* [1983] 1 W.L.R. 927 Ch D. In *Re RA Noble (Clothing) Ltd* [1983] B.C.L.C. 273, however, Nourse J held that a course of conduct resulting in "the exclusion of [a joint venturer] from participation in all major decisions affecting the Company's affairs" amounted to conduct prejudicial to the interests of the joint venturer. In *Re Company (No.00477 of 1986)* (1986) 2 B.C.C. 99171, Hoffmann J endorsed this trend

by holding that a joint venturer might have a legitimate expectation as a member to be employed by the company as a director. To the same effect are the judgments of the same judge in *Re A Company (No.007623 of 1984)* [1986] B.C.L.C. 362 Ch D (Comp); and *Re Company (No.004377 of 1986)* [1987] 1 W.L.R. 102 Ch D. This line of authority has been endorsed in the *Saul D Harrison* case and *O'Neill v Phillips* [1999] 1 W.L.R. 1092, although it has been held in the latter case that the label "legitimate expectation" is inappropriate and that such expectations should not be allowed to lead a life of their own, since such an expectation is merely the correlative right in a minority shareholder arising out of the enforceability in equity of the real bargain between shareholders (at 1102). See also *Re A Company (No.007623 of 1984)* [1986] B.C.L.C. 362; *Re DR Chemicals* [1989] 5 B.C.C. 39.

Justification for exclusion

Replace first paragraph with:

In "exclusion" cases, the majority may seek to justify the exclusion of the minority as being a reasonable management decision, taken in the best commercial interests of the business. It is clear, however, that it is not sufficient that the majority were acting in good faith and making a reasonable commercial decision: *Re Westbourne Galleries* [1973] A.C. 360 at 381F–H. But it still remains open to the majority to argue that the "working partner" has brought his exclusion upon himself by reason of his own misconduct. Given that the statutory test is ultimately unfairness and it is necessary to take into account the conduct of both parties,[95] as a matter of common sense any misconduct by the excluded party would at least be a factor to be taken into account by the court in deciding whether the majority has acted unfairly and also what, if any, relief to grant. But, in order to do practical justice, the courts are loathe to allow s.994 petitioners to degenerate into old-style divorce cases, where one side blames the other, the proceedings become lengthy and expensive, and at the end of the day the court has the very difficult and often futile task of deciding where fault lies in circumstances where the parties have simply fallen out and neither side is seriously at fault.[96] Lord Hoffmann said in *O'Neill v Phillips* [1999] 1 W.L.R. 1092 at 1104 and 1107:

7-142

> "There are cases, such as A *Company, Re (No.006834 of 1988), Ex p. Kremer* [1989] B.C.L.C. 365, in which it has been said that if a breakdown in relations has caused the majority to remove a shareholder from participation in the management, it is usually a waste of time to try to investigate who caused the breakdown. Such breakdowns often occur (as in this case) without either side having done anything seriously wrong or unfair. It is not fair to the excluded member, who will usually have lost his employment, to keep his assets locked in the company … .
>
> The Law Commission *Report on Shareholder Remedies*, pp.30–37, paras 3.26–56[97] has recommended that in a private company limited by shares in which substantially all the members are directors, there should be a statutory presumption that the removal of a shareholder as a director, or from substantially all his functions as a director, is unfairly prejudicial conduct. This does not seem to me very different in practice from the present law."[98]

In *R&H Electric v Haden Bill Electrical* [1995] B.C.C. 958, Robert Walker J, after referring to the judgment of Lord Templeman in *Tay Bok Choon v Tahanson Sdn Bhd* [1987] 1 W.L.R. 413, held (at 295):

> "Lord Templeman qualified the expectation of the petitioner in that case by limiting it to the period until 'for some other reason a change in management and control became necessary'; and that qualification is no doubt appropriate in any similar case, including the present case. The personal troubles between Mr Pitt and Mr Watkins (which were acknowledged but not investigated in the course of cross-examination of Mr Pitt) made it inevitable that there should be a change in management and control, and Mr Watkins' alliance with the Hoggs (an unlikely event, viewed from 1989) made it inevitable that Mr Pitt should be the one to go, regardless of the rights and wrongs of the personal troubles. Conversely, however unmeritorious Mr Pitt's personal conduct, it could not in my judg-

ment justify the majority shareholders in summarily ejecting him without consultation or discussion about the future of Mr Pitt's equity capital, and R & H's loan capital, in Haden Bill. It was largely for that reason that I would have rejected any suggestion (which was only mentioned, and not pressed) that the personal troubles should be investigated by recall of witnesses and further cross-examination.

Had the position been considered and discussed between the majority shareholders and Mr Pitt in February 1994, I think the solution likely to have emerged, and a fair solution, would have been that Mr Pitt should cease to be chairman and a director of Haden Bill, that his shares should be bought by the majority shareholders without a discount for its being a minority holding, and that R & H's loans to Haden Bill should be repaid as soon as reasonably possible (either by refinancing or out of retained profits, but in any event substantially sooner than if the minimum instalments fixed by the deed of April 5, 1993 had continued)."

In *O'Neill v Phillips*, the House of Lords endorsed this approach which recognised commercial realities in the event of a breakdown of relations. Compare the grounds upon which a court may take into account the misconduct of the petitioner in refusing or crafting relief in para.7-200 et seq. In *Sheikh v Ijaz* [2018] EWHC 1693 (Ch), ICC Judge Jones cited paras 7-142–7-143 with approval. In *Pinfold v Ansell* [2017] 2 B.C.L.C. 489 it was held that a director's expressed desire to step back from day-to-day management did not justify his exclusion. In *Re Edwardian Group Ltd* [2018] EWHC 1715 (Ch), Fancourt J held:

"412. ... [A] number of authorities establish that, in certain circumstances, the removal of a quasi-partner without making such an offer can be objectively justified. Those circumstances are, essentially, where the quasi-partner has brought his removal on himself by conduct that objectively justified the other members in excluding him in that way: see per Nourse J in *Re R.A. Noble & Sons (Clothing) Ltd* [1983] BCLC 273 at 292.

413. Lack or loss of competence in business affairs, a breakdown of the relationship of trust and confidence and even personal misbehaviour do not of themselves justify exclusion without a fair offer. The court does not indulge in what Lord Hoffmann once referred to as a 'contest of virtue'. Nor can removal without a fair offer be justified solely on the grounds of what the majority consider to be in the best interests of the company: per Lord Wilberforce in *Ebrahimi* at p.381.

414. In *Re a company No. 002470 of 1988, ex p. Nicholas* [1992] BCC 895, Harman J held that the exclusion of a quasi-partner was not unfair where the partner was responsible for friction and difficulties in the conduct of the company's business such that management relations had broken down. In *Woolwich v Milne* [2003] EWHC 414 (Ch), Sir Donald Rattee held that Mr Woolwich was not unfairly excluded where, by doing specific matters that he had previously agreed not to do, he placed the efficient conduct of the business of the Company in jeopardy and posed 'a significant threat to the future well-being of the company's business' (p.48).

415. The authorities do not establish any bright line between what does and does not justify exclusion without an offer, but it is clear that the conduct in question must be misconduct in the affairs of the company, not merely personal misconduct. It must be so serious as to undermine the basis for the equitable considerations that bound the parties. The right approach, in my judgment, is to ask whether the exclusion without a fair offer is proportionate and justified by the misconduct in question, but bearing in mind that incompetence, mere misconduct and a breakdown of confidence are not sufficient to justify removal without a fair offer."

[95] In a partnership, partners owe mutual duties of good faith: para.7-104.

[96] See *Re RA Noble (Clothing) Ltd* [1983] B.C.L.C. 273 for a different approach. The essence of the allegation of unfair prejudice was that one joint-venturer had been excluded from involvement in the major decisions of the company. Nourse J considered the lengthy and detailed evidence. He observed (at 292):

"... I do not think that it can be said that [the respondent's] conduct was unfairly prejudicial to the interests of [the petitioner]. In my judgment, the crucial word on the facts of this case is 'unfairly.'

It is at this point that [the petitioner's] disinterest becomes a decisive factor. In the end ... I do not think that a reasonable bystander, observing the consequences of [the respondent's] conduct and judging it to have been prejudicial to the interests of [the Petitioner], would regard it as having been unfair. I think he would say that [the Petitioner] had partly brought it upon himself. That means that there is no case for relief under section 75."

[97] The Law Commission recommended the inclusion in Table A of a shareholders' exit article, in the form set out in Appendix 1. That recommendation was not acted upon. Paragraph 5.49 of the Report states:

"To summarise, we recommend that a shareholders' exit article should be included in Table A, setting out a mechanism by which shareholders can require their shares to be purchased in certain agreed circumstances. Whilst the regulation should set out a framework for the exercise of these exit rights, it should require the shareholders to make positive choices (notably in relation to the events triggering the rights, the basis of valuation and the choice of the valuer) in order to bring the regulation into effect."

[98] See the same sentiments expressed by Lord Hoffmannin *Re Company (No.007623 of 1984)* [1986] B.C.L.C. 362 at 366; *Re Company (No.006834 of 1988) Ex p. Kremer* (1989) 5 B.C.C. 218; *Re Company (No.004377 of 1986)* [1987] 1 W.L.R. 102. Contrast the earlier approach in *RA Noble* (see fn.96 above).

Parallel Employment Tribunal proceedings

Replace "Wootliff v Rushton-Turner [2016] EWHC 2802 (Ch)" with:
Wootliff v Rushton-Turner [2018] 1 B.C.L.C. 48

7-146

Excessive remuneration and inadequate dividends

Excessive remuneration

To the end of the paragraph, add:
The issue of excessive remuneration and inadequate dividends has been considered in several recent cases.

7-153

In *Pinfold v Ansell* [2017] 2 B.C.L.C. 489 the court applied the test of the market rate for the work and skills in question and determined that payments above that rate were unfairly prejudicial.

In *Re CF Booth Ltd* [2017] EWHC 457 (Ch) the court applied the test set out in *Irvine v Irvine*, namely whether, applying "objective commercial criteria", the remuneration taken by the directors was within the bracket that they would expect to receive, and concluded that the remuneration far exceeded the amount that reasonable directors acting in the ebst interests of the company could have thought fair remuneration. As to the complaint that the dividend policy of the company was unfair, the court held that the issue was whether the directors had complied with their duties in determining the dividend policy: [76]. On the facts, including their excessive remuneration, their desire to acquire minority shareholdings, and the fact that the company managed to afford to spend considerable sums of money on the provision of luxuries for the directors, it was held that the directors acted in breach of their duties in adopting a no-dividend policy. In so doing, the learned judge, at [91], approved and applied the following passage in para.7-165:

"Nevertheless, if the remuneration that is voted is plainly in excess of the market value of those services, then the court will be likely to infer that the remuneration is a dressed-up return of capital and hence unfairly prejudicial to the minority who are excluded from it. If the controlling directors or shareholders pay themselves remuneration not by reference to a proper reward for services rendered but as a disguised payment of a discriminatory dividend, then such conduct would be unfairly prejudicial to the interests of those members who were not directors. In the oft-cited judgement of Oliver J in *Re Halt Garage (1964) Ltd* [1982] 3 All E.R. 1016 Ch D, the learned judge summarised the underlying principles as follows: ..."

7-154 *To the end of the paragraph, add:*
The general principle is that a director, as a trustee, could be allowed to profit from his office only so far as the articles of association permitted: *Ball v Hughes* [2018] B.C.C. 196.

7-165 *To the end of the paragraph, add:*
See *Re Edwardian Group Ltd* [2018] EWHC 1715 (Ch), at [529]–[562].

Loss of confidence in management

7-169 *To the end of the paragraph, add:*
In *Pinfold v Ansell* [2017] 2 B.C.L.C. 489 a complaint of serious mismanagement was rejected—there was no more than disagreement between shareholders as to the best commercial course of action.

Procedural irregularity

7-172 *To the end of the paragraph, add:*
See *Re Edwardian Group Ltd* [2018] EWHC 1715 (Ch), where it was held that a breach of fiduciary duty by the directors, such as not to place themselves in a position of conflict of personal interest and duty, or a biased investigation, could amount to unfair prejudice merely because it was "corrosive of good administration and trust between shareholders and directors": [339], [493], [606], [620].

EXIT ROUTES UNDER ARTICLES OF ASSOCIATION AND SHAREHOLDERS' AGREEMENTS

7-194 *To the end of the paragraph, add:*
In *Gray v Braid Group (Holdings)* [2016] CSIH 68, where *Re LCM Wealth Management Ltd* was cited, it was held that it was open to a judge to apply the "bad leaver" and hence expropriatory (valuation at par) provisions in the articles of association in determining the value of the shares of a petitioner who had established unfair prejudice. The court had found the petitioner guilty of gross misconduct, and that such misconduct entitled the respondents to trigger those "bad leaver" provisions, even though they had not done so yet. Hence, the "fair" price for the petitioner's shares was the price that would have been arrived at by the operation of those provisions, i.e. par value.

ARBITRATION CLAUSES

7-198 *Replace paragraph 7-198 with:*
The shareholders can lawfully agree to submit their disputes to arbitration and the fact that the dispute is one which would fall within the jurisdiction of court under ss.994–6 is no reason why the arbitration agreement should not be enforced according to its terms: *Fulham Football Club (1987) Ltd v Richards* [2012] Ch. 333; *Exeter City AFC Ltd v Football Conference Ltd* [2004] 1 W.L.R. 2910 overruled. It appears that this remains even if, because the arbitrator's powers are more limited than the court's powers under the statutory remedy, this leaves the minority shareholder with no effective remedy.[123] *Ghossoub v Team Y&R Holdings Hong Kong Ltd* [2016] HKEC 1341, noted in fn.123, has been upheld on appeal: [2017] HKEC 1532—*Fulham* was distinguished by the HK Court of Appeal on the basis that the petitioner in the case before it had no equivalent remedy in the English court favoured by the exclusive jurisdiction clause or indeed any court other than the

"CLEAN HANDS" AND MISCONDUCT 35

Hong Kong courts—only the HK courts had jurisdiction to determine the petition for unfair prejudice—that factor provided strong grounds for not enforcing an exclusive jurisdiction clause: [32].

[123] The point did not arise in the *Fulham Football Club (1987) v Richards* case. The Court of Appeal's answer was that the risk that the arbitration proceedings did not provide an adequate remedy would fall on the wronged shareholder: [84]. Longmore LJ suggested that the arbitrator would have the same powers as the court would have under statute: [96]. The *Fulham Football Club (1987) v Richards* decision was not enthusiastically received in *Ghossoub v Team Y&R Holdings Hong Kong Ltd* [2016] HKEC 1341.

"CLEAN HANDS" AND MISCONDUCT ON THE PART OF THE PETITIONER

To the end of the paragraph, add:
Compare the grounds upon which a court may take into account the misconduct of the petitioner as a justification for exclusion in para.7-142 et seq.

7-200

To the end of the paragraph, add:
In *Interactive Technology Corp v Ferster* [2016] EWHC 2896 (Ch) at [318], Morgan J held:

7-202

> "In considering whether the matters of complaint were unfairly prejudicial to [the petitioner], I have not sought to weigh in the scales the wrongdoing of Jonathan in relation to ITC against the prejudicial conduct of ITC, Warren and Stuart. It is established that wrongdoing on the part of a petitioner seeking relief under section 994 can be relevant in two ways. The first way is that the petitioner's wrongdoing may make the prejudicial conduct of the respondent not unfair. The second way is that the petitioner's wrongdoing may justify the court in refusing to grant relief to the petitioner or may influence the choice of any relief which is granted. These propositions are established by *Re London School of Electronics Ltd* [1986] Ch 211 at 222 B-C, *Richardson v Blackmore* [2006] BCC 276 and *Grace v Biagioli* [2006] BCC 85." [318]—applied in *Corran v Butters* [2017] EWHC 2294 (Ch), at [117]–[118, [312]; *Re Edwardian Group Ltd* [2018] EWHC 1715 (Ch), at [616].

The above statement of principle (which corresponds with the statement of principle in the first sentence of para.7-200) does not claim to be anything other than a restatement of what Nourse J said in *Re London School of Electronics Ltd* at 222B, nor to detract from the principle, derived from *Richardson v Blackmore*, that a court does not sit under a palm tree in exercising its discretion and the equitable principle of clean hands remains useful guidance upon the issue of whether and what relief should be granted having regard to the petitioner's misconduct.

A good example of the relevance of a petitioner's misconduct to the fairness of the remedy, and of the connection between the two, is *Gray v Braid Group (Holdings)* [2016] CSIH 68, where it was held that it was open to a judge to apply the "bad leaver" and hence expropriatory (valuation at par) provisions in the articles of association in determining the value of the shares of a petitioner who had established unfair prejudice. The court had found the petitioner guilty of gross misconduct, and that such misconduct entitled the respondents to trigger those "bad leaver" provisions, even though they had not done so yet. Hence, the "fair" price for the petitioner's shares was the price that would have been arrived at by the operation of those provisions, i.e. par value. In other words, although the court did not so state expressly, there was an "immediate and necessary relation" (as per *Richardson v Blackmore*) between the petitioner's misconduct and the remedy granted.

In *Corran v Butters* [2017] EWHC 2294 (Ch), at [117]–[118], [312], paras 7-200–7-201 were approved and applied.

In *Harbour Front Ltd v Leung Yuet Keung* [2018] HKEC 334, HKCFI, Harris J declined to grant a winding up order on the just and equitable basis where the petitioner had been justifiably excluded from management and had subsequently failed to remedy its own misconduct, even though subsequent acts of misconduct on the part of the majority were made out. In reaching this conclusion, the learned judge criticised at [43] the statement of principle in the first sentence of para.7-202, namely "the petitioner's misconduct is relevant if it has an immediate and necessary relation to the unfairly prejudicial conduct of which complaint is made as wrongly", as wrongly suggesting that "misconduct must in some way be connected to the unfairly prejudicial conduct". But that statement has to be read as part of the whole of paras 7-200–7-203. The statement is derived from the judgment of Lloyd LJ in *Blackmore v Richardson* cited in para.7-203, to the effect that the equitable doctrine of clean hands provided useful guidance by analogy (but no more). The learned judge's conclusion at [44] may be understood as an entirely uncontroversial finding that the majority's misconduct, subsequent to the petitioner's exclusion, was not sufficiently serious to justify a winding up order in all the circumstances, including the failure of the petitioner's main complaint of having been wrongfully excluded from management. If however his judgment is understood as a finding that the petitioner should be deprived of relief because of his own misconduct (presumably in not remedying the reasons for its original exclusion from management), notwithstanding it was entirely unrelated to the established unfair prejudice, then this may not be consistent with English authorities such as *Blackmore v Richardson*.

Replace paragraph 7-204 with:

7-204 Abuse of the process of the court may also be taken into account by the court. In *Arrow Nominees v Blackledge* [2000] C.P. Rep. 59,[125] the Court of Appeal, in highly unusual circumstances, struck out a petition on the ground that one of the petitioners was persisting in his object of frustrating a fair trial. Ward LJ emphasised the impact of the CPR, which he described as the "apotheosis" of the ideals that access to the courts was open to all but the time of the courts was a precious resource which needed to be managed fairly in order to be fair to all: at 200e–f. He described the petitioner's conduct as (at 202d)

> "a flagrant and continuing affront to the court. Striking out is not a disproportionate remedy for such an abuse, even when the petitioners lose so much of the fruits of their labour".

Applying *Henderson v Henderson* (1843) 3 Hare 100 principles, it is an abuse of process to pursue in a s.994 petition issues which either were or could and should have been determined in a previous petition: *Re Falmouth House Freehold Co Ltd* [2017] EWHC 674 (Ch).

[125] See *Masood v Zahoor* [2010] 1 W.L.R. 746 and *Summers v Fairclough Homes Ltd* [2012] 1 W.L.R. 2004.

DELAY AND ACQUIESCENCE

To the end of the paragraph, add:

7-205 In *Re Edwardian Group Ltd* [2018] EWHC 1715 (Ch), Fancourt J held:

> "In my judgment, the right approach is to consider how the delay in question should affect the exercise of the court's discretion under section 996 to make such order as it thinks fit. There is no statutory time limit for issuing a petition, nor does the equitable doctrine of laches strictly apply where the relief sought is not equitable relief. However, unjusti-

fied delay resulting in prejudice or an irretrievable change of position (the essential ingredients of a defence of laches) are likely to be significant factors in the exercise of the court's discretion to grant or refuse a particular remedy. So too is any evidence that the Petitioners have previously acquiesced in the state of affairs of which they now complain, which is the basis of a number of the authorities to which I was referred. If, in view of the delay and the reasons for the delay, it is unfair or inappropriate in all the circumstances for the Petitioners to obtain the relief that they seek, the Court will exercise its discretion to refuse it." ([571].)

In that case it was possible and proportionate to allow for culpable delay by fixing the valuation date at an earlier date: [607], [632]–[636].

CHAPTER 8

Unfair Prejudice 2: Remedies

TABLE OF CONTENTS

Final Order	8-01■
The Court's Powers and Discretion	8-09■
Orders in Favour of the Majority	8-32■
The Persons Against Whom Relief may be Granted	8-34■
Specific Remedies	8-42■
Offers to Buy Out at Independent Valuation	8-72■
Interim Injunctive Relief	8-105■
Valuation of Shares	8-128■
Alternative Remedies	8-184

FINAL ORDER

Jurisdiction

To the end of the paragraph, add:
   Where the defence to a s.994 petition has been struck out, the petitioner still had to satisfy the court with evidence that relief should be granted to him: *Re Bankside Hotels Ltd* [2018] EWHC 1035 (Ch).

   Paragraphs 8-01–8-08 were cited with approval in *Lai Chi Keung v Wang Zhihua* [2018] HKEC 1004 for the proposition that the court does not have jurisdiction, even by consent, to make an order for the buy-out of shares until it is satisfied that there has been unfairly prejudicial conduct. In that case the process could not be truncated because the parties had not agreed the terms of the buy-out and so an expedited trial was ordered.

8-01

To the end of the paragraph, add:
   It is considered that the court has jurisdiction from an early stage to direct a valuation of the company with a view to settlement or the narrowing of issues: see the notes under paras 8-168 and 9-32.

8-04

THE COURT'S POWERS AND DISCRETION

Powers

To the end of the paragraph, add:
   In *Rembert v Daniel* [2018] EWHC 388 (Ch) it was held that the court had power under s.996 to award a petitioner equitable compensation to compensate him for the wrongful disposal of the company's assets and the consequential diminution in value of his investment. The learned judge appreciated the argument that this

8-14

breached the rule against granting a shareholder damages for the company's loss but does not appear to have considered the interests of creditors.

In *Re ASA Resource Group Plc* [2018] EWHC 1102 (Ch), the court declined to strike out a petition seeking damages and equitable compensation for a tortious conspiracy to injure the petitioners by unlawful means. The petitioners had sold their shares, but claimed that the sale price was reduced by the unfairly prejudicial conduct and to seek relief for the benefit of the purchasers.

Discretion

To the end of the paragraph, add:

8-18 A good example of the relevance and relation of a petitioner's misconduct to the fairness of the remedy is *Gray v Braid Group (Holdings)* [2016] CSIH 68, where it was held that it was open to a judge to apply the "bad leaver" and hence expropriatory (valuation at par) provisions in the articles of association in determining the value of the shares of a petitioner who had established unfair prejudice. The court had found the petitioner guilty of gross misconduct, and that such misconduct entitled the respondents to trigger those "bad leaver" provisions, even though they had not done so yet. Hence, the "fair" price for the petitioner's shares was the price that would have been arrived at by the operation of those provisions, i.e. par value.

To the end of the paragraph, add:

8-28 See *Corran v Butters* [2017] EWHC 2294 (Ch), at [117]–[118], [312], [317] for a case where the court found unfair prejudice, made an order which remedied it, but declined to make a share purchase order.

To the end of the paragraph, add:

8-29 See *VB Football Assets v Blackpool Football Club (Properties) Ltd* [2017] EWHC 2767 (Ch): circumstances were such that a buy-out order was the only appropriate remedy: [445]–[455].

The material time

Replace paragraph 8-30 with:

8-30 The relevant time for determining whether an order should be made under s.994 is the date of hearing of the petition, not the date of its presentation: *Grace v Biagioli* [2006] B.C.C. 85 at [73].[16] Accordingly, conduct after the presentation of the petition and before the hearing may be relied upon in support of the petition. However, in *Cheung Hon Wah v Cheung Kam Wah* [2005] HKEC 765 it was held that, by analogy with other ordinary actions (the *Eshelby* rule), amendments should not generally be allowed in respect of new matters which had arisen since the presentation of the petition and did not arise out of already pleaded causes of action. The better course was for the petitioner to issue a fresh petition. *Sed quaere* as to whether the *Eshelby* rule, which is concerned with fresh causes of action, applies to unfair prejudice petitions. In *Re Hailey Group Ltd*,[17] the petitioner had originally sought an order that the respondents sell their shares to him but, following the appointment of administrative receivers, sought instead an order that the respondents purchase his shares. It was held that he was not entitled to such an order, since it would be tantamount to imposing a fine on the respondents. The learned judge envisaged circumstances where supervening insolvency would not prevent the making of such an order, for example where the unfairly prejudicial conduct had prevented the petitioner from selling his shares at a proper price prior to the onset of insolvency. If a petitioner is entitled to an order that his shares be purchased and the appropriate date of valuation is before the onset of insolvency, the onset of insolvency should be irrelevant, save possibly as relevant to the issue of valuation.

[16] The same principle applies to winding up on the just and equitable basis: *Jenkins v Supascaf* [2006] 3 N.Z.L.R. 264.

[17] *Re Hailey Group Ltd* [1992] B.C.C. 542 Ch D. See also *Re Fildes Bros* [1970] 1 All E.R. 923 Ch D at 927d.

ORDERS IN FAVOUR OF THE MAJORITY

To the end of the paragraph, add:
It appears that a majority shareholder who has sufficient shares to procure the passing of a special resolution to alter the articles may amend the articles so as to empower the company to buy out the shares of a minority shareholder provided that he does so in good faith in the interests of the company: see para.5-50.

8-32

THE PERSONS AGAINST WHOM RELIEF MAY BE GRANTED

To the end of the paragraph, add:
Where a share purchase order is considered appropriate, it will frequently be made against the company itself.

8-34

To the end of the paragraph, add:
In *Re Pedersen (Thameside) Ltd* [2018] B.C.C. 58, the court struck out a petition as against a respondent against whom it was not alleged that he was involved in the unfairly prejudicial conduct complained of.

8-35

To the end of the paragraph, add:
In *Re TPD Investments Ltd* [2017] EWHC 657 (Ch) the court declined to grant relief against certain directors on the ground that there were insufficient factors to render it just to impose liability on them: [161].
In *Re Edwardian Group Ltd* [2018] EWHC 1715 (Ch), Fancourt J held:

8-37

"The Petitioners rely on the cases of *F&C Alternative Investments (Holdings) Ltd v Barthelemy* [2011] EWHC 1731 (Ch); [2012] Ch 613 and *Apex Global Ltd v Fi Call Ltd* [2013] EWHC 1652 (Ch); [2014] BCC 286. In both cases the relevant criterion for the grant of relief against a respondent was identified as being whether what was done involved unfairness in which the relevant person was sufficiently implicated, or to which he was so closely connected, as to warrant relief being granted against him." [628].

SPECIFIC REMEDIES

Share purchase orders (in general)

To the end of the paragraph, add:
In *Re TPD Investments Ltd* [2017] EWHC 657 (Ch) the court allowed the respondents a reasonable time in which to realize assets in order to buy the petitioner's shares: [146].

8-48

OFFERS TO BUY OUT AT INDEPENDENT VALUATION

(1) Basis of valuation

Replace paragraph 8-91 with:

8-91 If it is to be held that the petitioner is unreasonably rejecting an offer to buy him out, the offered basis of valuation (e.g. going concern or break-up, with or without discount for a minority shareholding) must be the best that the petitioner could reasonably expect to achieve at a full hearing. This will usually mean that the offer will have to concede no discount for a minority shareholding: see *O'Neill v Phillips* at para.8-82 above. But, when it comes to trial and the final relief that a court may grant, see para.8-134 et seq, particularly para.8-149 et seq. See *Re Edwardian Group Ltd* [2018] EWHC 1715 (Ch), noted under para.8-158 below. There is a presumption in practice in favour of a valuation of a business on the going-concern basis, where that is more favourable to the petitioner: see paras 8-134 et seq. below.

(4) Costs of the proceedings

To the end of the paragraph, add:

8-97 The ability of the court to determine the issue of costs independently of the issue of liability has been addressed in many English cases in contexts other than the unfair prejudice remedy. The position may depend upon whether or not the claimant has served a notice of discontinuance.

In *Messih v McMillan Williams* [2010] 6 Costs L.R. 914, CA the claimant sued two defendants, LMA and MH, for negligence and LMA served a contribution notice on MH. The claimant settled with LMA. MH refused to settle with the claimant on the basis of no order as to costs but the claimant "nonetheless went ahead and served notice of his discontinuance of his claim against them" (at [14] per Patten LJ). It was held that the general presumption applied, namely that MH was entitled to its costs, and it was no answer for the claimant to say that he would have succeeded at trial against MH. The critical feature was the fact that the claimant had sought to avoid a trial on liability:

> "30 No judge encourages litigation about costs and a major theme of the CPR is the avoidance of unnecessary disputes and the costs which they can generate. But the *avoidance of the costs of a trial* is the necessary consequence of any discontinuance and cannot, of itself, justify a departure from the normal rule that the discontinuing party pays the other side's costs up to the date of discontinuance. There has to be something more than that to justify that departure. Otherwise the normal rule would be displaced in every case.
>
> 31 In this case there was nothing more. As already mentioned, the claimant knew what MW's position was and that it wished to contest its liability for the claim. The claimant made his decision to discontinue notwithstanding this and in the knowledge that the settlement with LMA made no provision for the payment of MW's costs against the claimant as opposed to those of the third party proceedings. By doing so Mr Messih *removed the ability of MW to establish its defence* and left the court in the position of being unable to determine what the outcome of the trial is likely to have been. The circumstances were therefore the quite usual consequences of a decision to discontinue and I can see nothing in them to justify the order which the Recorder made." Per Patten LJ with emphasis added.

See also *Nelson's Yard Management Co v Eziefula* [2013] C.P. Rep. 29 at [31] per Beatson LJ.

However, there is a distinction between discontinuance and the situation where a claimant has obtained all or substantially all the relief which he sought and asks the court to determine costs: *Winchester Park Ltd v Sehayek* [2016] EWHC 1216 (QB) per Garnham J at [25]–[34]: in particular:

> "30 There was no discontinuance here. Instead, the Respondent invited the Judge to dismiss the claim on the basis that he had obtained the relief he sought, namely the restoration of the lift service. Continuation of the claim would have been pointless. That is, as a matter of both form and substance, entirely different from discontinuance. In those circumstances, the approach indicated in *Nelson's Yard* is inapplicable.
>
> 31 Instead, the costs were at large and it was a matter for the Judge to determine the appropriate costs order. The merits of the claim were potentially relevant to the exercise of discretion on costs."

Courts have been prepared to determine the outstanding issue of costs in such circumstances, with appropriate directions to limit the investigation of the facts and underlying merits of the case: see *Hanspaul v Ward* [2016] EWHC 1358 (Ch) at [16]–[23]; *Hanspaul v Ward* unreported, 9 March 2017 at [14] per Chief Master Marsh.

INTERIM INJUNCTIVE RELIEF

Generally

To the end of the paragraph, add:

8-114 In *Shih Hua Investment Co Ltd v Zhang Aidong* [2017] HKEC 88, the court, whilst acknowledging that the power to make such an order was to be sparingly exercised, made by way of interim injunctive relief an order replacing the existing directors of a solvent and profitable business with suitable independent professionals, rather than appointing provisional liquidators or receivers

Appointment of receivers or provisional liquidators

Replace paragraph 8-123 with:

8-123 Similarly, the appointment of a provisional liquidator to a trading company is a most serious step for a court to take; where, however, it is likely that the petition (seeking winding up, alone or in the alternative to relief on the unfair prejudice ground) will succeed[52] and the assets are at risk of dissipation and need to be protected so as to preserve the relief that the petitioner is seeking, then the court may appoint a provisional liquidator under s.135 of the Insolvency Act 1986[53] and this is in general preferable to injunctive relief freezing the assets of the company: *Revenue and Customs Commissioners v Rochdale Drinks Distributors Ltd* [2013] 1 B.C.C. 419 (a case concerning an insolvent company). For earlier authorities, see e.g. *Re Union Accident Insurance Co* [1972] 1 All E.R. 1105 Ch D; *Re Highfield Commodities Ltd* [1985] 1 W.L.R. 149 Ch D; *Re A Company (No.003102 of 1991) Ex p. Nyckeln Finance Co* [1991] B.C.L.C. 539. The cases on the appointment of provisional liquidators in the context of creditors' petitions are replete with references to the applicant having to establish the "need" for such an appointment, i.e. the court had to consider alternative less intrusive solutions to the problems before making such an appointment. The issue was pithily expressed by Megarry V.C. in *Re Highfield Commodities* [1985] 1 W.L.R. 149, when he said that the appointment of a provisional liquidator "may have serious consequences for the company, and so a need for the exercise of the power must overtop those consequences."

For the ultimate responsibility for the costs of a provisional liquidation, see *Re Beppler & Jacobson Ltd* [2016] EWHC 20 (Ch), reversed on appeal to the Court of Appeal: [2018] EWCA Civ 763 (on 16 July 2018 the Supreme Court refused permission to appeal).

[52] In cases concerned with creditors' petitions, the relief in question is a final winding-up order. In the context of contributories' petitions, winding up order is a last resort, the court being more likely to grant lesser relief under the unfair prejudice remedy, such as a share purchase order.

[53] Contrast this wide power with the power under s.104 of the Cayman Islands Companies Law (2012 Revision) which spells out the broad purposes for which such an order may be made—but NB in the Cayman Islands, relief on the unfair prejudice ground is not free-standing but, as it were, parasitic upon the right to a winding up order.

Freezing orders

Replace second paragraph with:

8-126 There appears to be no reason in principle why, in an appropriate case,[56] if a freezing order is sought against the assets of the respondent individuals in a petition, the requisite cause of action against them should not be pleaded and pursued in the petition itself. An unfair prejudice petition may be an appropriate proceeding to seek compensation or other relief in respect of misappropriation of company assets. Furthermore, where the petitioner seeks an order that the majority buys the petitioner out, and the majority threaten to dissipate their assets and those of the company in order to frustrate such an order, it would be odd if the court had no jurisdiction to make a freezing order against the majority shareholder. It is clear that, notwithstanding the decision in *Re Premier Electronics (GB) Ltd* [2002] B.C.C. 911 Ch D, the court does have power to grant a freezing order to protect the company's assets pending the hearing of the petition: per Briggs J in *Revenue and Customs Commissioners v Egleton* [2007] B.C.C. 78 at [16]–[17]; *Reiner v Gershinson* [2004] 2 B.C.L.C. 376 at [102]. In *Palmer v Loveland* unreported, 16 August 2017 (Warren J) the court, applying observations made by Briggs J in *Revenue and Customs Commissioners v Egleton* [2007] B.C.C. 78, held that it had jurisdiction to grant freezing injunctions in the context of a s.994 petition to prevent dissipation of the assets of the company and of the third party recipients of the allegedly misappropriated company funds.

[56] See para.8-14 above.

VALUATION OF SHARES

Replace first paragraph with:

8-128 This is a very wide and specialist subject, on which one would be tempted to defer to the expertise of share valuers. This temptation is to be resisted, however, because there are questions of law and principle involved in the present context, and it must always be borne in mind that share valuation is an art not a science (*Joiner v George* [2003] B.C.C. 298) and a court retains a wide freedom to disregard the views of experts and apply the court's view of what is fair and sensible in all the circumstances: *Re Planet Organic Ltd* [2000] B.C.C. 610 Ch D. The courts have recently deprecated the emergence of a new breed of professional expert valuers whose principal experience lies in acting as an expert witness. The view of an expert valuer will generally carry greater weight with the court if it is supported by objective evidence in the form of personal practical experience in buying and selling business of the type in question, in other words the experience to be found in the corporate finance department: see *Re Sunrise Radio Ltd* [2011] EWHC 3821 (Ch) at [5]:

> "[H], when I asked her what her practical experience was of advising on actual dealings in the marketplace, candidly acknowledged that she had none as that was the function of her corporate finance department. [Counsel] explained to me that people who were dealing in the marketplace had, as it were, got fed up with being beaten up by barristers and judges and hence the emergence of a breed of experts. I acknowledge that such a breed is now common but I deprecate the development of people whose primary expertise is in giving evidence, rather than the practical application of that expertise. It seems to me that the court would ordinarily in a case such as this find more helpful the evidence of someone who has actually (if I can put it in the vernacular) got their hands dirty in the marketplace by advising clients in the real world of acquisition and merger activity."

Much will depend upon the expert valuation evidence that is adduced in a case so care must be taken in deriving any points of general principle from decided cases: see *Wann v Birkinshaw* [2017] EWCA Civ 84 at [41]. Further, in that case emphasis was placed on the expertise of the valuer in giving evidence as to what the outcome of negotiations in an arm's length sale would have been. See also *Re Edwardian Group Ltd* [2018] EWHC 1715 (Ch) at [651]–[652], discussed further under para.8-158 below.

Replace paragraph 8-131 with:
In the case of a minority stake in unquoted companies, however, there will be no or a very limited market for the stake.[58] Not only does this make it much more difficult to value the company as a whole, but it also means that minority stakes have no demonstrable commercial value in the sense that the shareholder is unlikely to have any means of realising them save by negotiation with the other shareholders or court order.[59] In *Re Edwardian Group Ltd* [2018] EWHC 1715 (Ch) at [651]–[652], Fancourt J held that the "fair" value for the minority shareholding was arrived at by adding to their "market value" one-half of the "marriage value" with the majority's shares, i.e. the additional value created by adding the minority to the majority shareholding. He reasoned that such a value reflected the likely outcome of arm's length negotiations. But *sed quaere*—he had no evidence before him as to how experts would assess the "market value", or the likely outcome of any arm's length sale negotiations, and had previously held that the shares were unsaleable in the open market due to the board's misconduct ([620]).

8-131

[58] There is no such thing as a "reasonable price", or indeed an "open market value" for shares in an unquoted company: *Gillatt v Sky Television Ltd* [2000] 2 B.C.L.C. 103 CA (Civ Div). But see *Blindley Heath Investments Ltd v Bass* [2015] EWCA Civ 1023, where a third party bought a minority stake.

[59] *Re Annacott Holdings* [2012] EWHC 1662 (Ch) at [67]–[68]. In that case, there appears to have been expert evidence on the lack of marketability of individual shareholdings, which must surely be irrelevant save in the context of assessing the appropriate discount for a minority shareholding (if applicable).

The basis of valuation

Replace second paragraph with:
There is, however, another way of approaching the valuation exercise, which is the method invariably adopted in the context of quoted shares, namely the dividend yield from the point of view of the individual shareholder. In *Re Blue Index* [2014] EWHC 2680 (Ch), the respondents' expert valuer favoured a dividend yield basis of valuation for the petitioner's very small, three per cent, shareholding. Since it was

8-134

accepted that a discount for a minority shareholding was inherent in such a valuation basis, and it was held in that case (see para.8-157 below) that a discount was inappropriate because the petitioner had paid more for his shares than reflected any value that could be put on them, this valuation basis was rejected in favour of the more usual whole-company capitalised earnings methodology. See *Re Watercor Ltd* [2017] EWHC 1814 (Ch) at [14], and para.8-10.

To the end of the paragraph, add:

8-136 See *Wann v Birkinshaw* [2017] EWCA Civ 84 at [41].

(i) Discount for a minority shareholding

To the end of the paragraph, add:

8-158 In *Re CF Booth Ltd* [2017] EWHC 457 (Ch) the learned judge considered *Irvine v Irvine* and *Re Sunrise Radio* in deciding whether a discount should be applied in the valuation of a minority shareholding. He does not seem to have been referred to *Re Blue Index*, probably because it was a family company where all the shareholders had inherited their shares from the company's founder and the petitioners were not involved in management. He held that the starting point was a discount but that, since there was in reality no such market, the discount likely to be obtained in an open market sale was not appropriate: following *CVC v Demarco Almeida*. He determined the discount at one-third for a 27% shareholding.

In *Re Edwardian Group Ltd* [2018] EWHC 1715 (Ch), Fancourt J was required to review the authorities as the application of a discount for a minority shareholding in the valuation of a petitioner's shares in circumstances which did not amount to a quasi-partnership. He began at [637] with the obiter dictum of Arden LJ (as she then was) in *Strahan v Wilcock* [2006] 2 B.C.L.C. 555 to the effect that it was difficult to conceive of circumstances in which a non-discounted basis of valuation would be appropriate in such circumstances. He noted the more recent cases of *Re Sunrise Radio Ltd* and *Re Blue Index Ltd*, noted in paras 8-157 and 8-158, where a discount was not applied because that would reward the majority whose wrongdoing had obliged the minority to seek a share purchase order. The learned judge held at [642] that there was no presumption in favour of no discount where the company is not a quasi-partnership, in contrast to the such a presumption where it was: the minority's shares never had any such enhanced value, and the petitioners were looking to sell their shares. He also noted at [647] that to apply an open market valuation, as the majority contended, would give them a very substantial windfall. Following an observation made by Pumfrey J in *Re Eurofinance Group Ltd* [2001] B.C.C. 551, a case where there was no market for the shares, he held at [651]–[652] that the "fair" value for the minority shareholding was arrived at by adding to the market value one-half of the "marriage value", i.e. the additional value created by adding the minority to the majority shareholding. He reasoned that such a value reflected the likely outcome of arm's length negotiations. *Sed quaere*. He does not appear to have had any evidence before him as to how experts would assess the "market value" and the outcome of any negotiations in an arm's length sale and had previously held that the shares were unsaleable in the open market due to the board's misconduct ([620]): see *Wann v Birkinshaw* [2017] EWCA Civ 84. He observed at [648] that the dictum of Arden LJ in *Strahan v Wilcock* did not imply that market value was the only alternative in cases where a non-discounted valuation was inappropriate.

(ii) Allowance for discrete assets or liabilities

To the end of the paragraph, add:
In *Wann v Birkinshaw* [2017] EWCA Civ 84 the Court of Appeal gave guidance as to what allowance should be made in a going-concern valuation for liabilities: there was no general principle and much depended upon the expert valuation evidence; in the circumstances of that case, there would have been a reduction in price for the company's liabilities in an arm's length sale, of approximately one half of the amount of the liabilities. See also *Re TFD Investments Ltd* [2017] EWHC 657 (Ch) where allowance was made for costs of sale of company assets: [122]–[124].

8-159

(iv) Date of valuation

To the end of the paragraph, add:
In *Re Edwardian Group Ltd* [2018] EWHC 1715 (Ch), Fancourt J held that it was possible and proportionate to allow for culpable delay on the part of the petitioner in commencing proceedings by fixing the valuation date at an earlier date: [607], [632]–[636].

8-163

To the end of the paragraph, add:
In *Pinfold v Ansell* [2017] 2 B.C.L.C. 489 the court held that the date of valuation should be the date of exclusion of the quasi-partner, because since then he had been locked into a business which was pursuing a commercial strategy from which he was excluded.
In *Re CF Booth Ltd* [2017] EWHC 457 (Ch) it was held that the date of valuation should be a date before the fall in value of a loss-making company.

8-164

To the end of the paragraph, add:
In *Re Watercor Ltd* [2017] EWHC 1814 (Ch) at [14] the court took into account evidence for a short period after the valuation date as to the level of business done with certain customers where it was in issue whether that business would have continued at the valuation date level.

8-165

The machinery of valuation

Replace first paragraph with:
The court can in the exercise of its wide case management powers at any stage order a valuation of the shares in issue—what it cannot do is to grant relief against any respondent on the basis of any such valuation until it is satisfied that the petition is well-founded: see para.8-02. Thus, Practice Note dated 22 April 2015 requires the parties to provide before the first directions hearing non-binding estimates of the value of the shares in issue so as to assist the court in meaningful costs management. This does not go as far as the practice in the Supreme Court of Victoria which envisages, at the earliest stage, the court making directions for the valuation of the shares and for a mediation, on the underlying assumption that commonly the dispute between the parties is the value of the shares, it being probable that one party will have to buy out the other: see the notes under para.9-32; and *Yung Yui Kwai v Yung Woon Kwai* [2017] HKEC 2824 at [7]. However, subject to being satisfied in that regard, it is clear that it should use its powers of case management under the CPR pro-actively in order to determine in a cost-effective manner what is often the main issue between the parties, although they may not admit as much on an open basis, namely the value of a particular shareholding, frequently the petitioner's. The costs of a full-blown valuation by the court, with experts instructed by both sides and cross-examined at length, are notoriously burdensome, and the

8-168

result is often liable to be unsatisfactory given the difficulty faced by the court in expressing its reasoning in terms of objective rational principles: see para.8-144 above. To put the issue another way, if there is inevitably an element of subjective assessment of the fair value, there is something to be said for the assessment being made by an expert, or by the court with the assiatance of a single joint expert, as cheaply as possible. On the other hand, the determination of the fair value remains a judicial task and no party is to be deprived of his right to a judicial determination of the fair value save for good reason.

Out-of-Court Valuations

To the end of the paragraph, add:

8-173 In *Gray v Braid Group (Holdings) Ltd* [2016] CSIH 68, it was held that it was open to a judge in the unusual circumstances of that case to apply the "bad leaver" and hence expropriatory (valuation at par) provisions in the articles of association in determining the value of the shares of a petitioner who had established unfair prejudice. The court had found the petitioner guilty of gross misconduct, and that such misconduct entitled the respondents to trigger those "bad leaver" provisions, even though they had not done so yet.

To the end of the paragraph, add:

8-178 See *Griffin v Wainwright* unreported, 18 August 2017, Chancery Division.

To the end of the paragraph, add:

8-182 *Cosmetic Warriors Ltd v Gerrie* [2015] EWHC 3718 (Ch) was upheld on appeal: [2017] 2 B.C.L.C. 456: there is no presumption in favour of a construction of pre-emption articles that a discount for a minority shareholding (as would be applied in an arm's length market sale) be applied.

CHAPTER 9

Unfair Prejudice 3: Practice and Procedure

TABLE OF CONTENTS

Locus Standi	9-01■
Pre-Action Disclosure	9-19
Pre-Action Protocols and the Chancery Guide	9-25
Procedure	9-30■
Strike-Out and Summary Judgment	9-55
Costs	9-65

LOCUS STANDI

To the end of the paragraph, add:
　See *Re AMT Coffee Ltd.* [2018] EWHC 1562 (Ch) for the steps that personal representatives need to take in order to acquire locus standi. **9-08**

To the end of the paragraph, add:
　In *Re ASA Resource Group Plc* [2018] EWHC 1102 (Ch), the court declined to strike out a petition seeking damages and equitable compensation for a tortious conspiracy to injure the petitioners by unlawful means. The petitioners had sold their shares, but claimed that the sale price was reduced by the unfairly prejudicial conduct and to seek relief for the benefit of the purchasers. **9-17**

PROCEDURE

Replace paragraph 9-30 with:
　The procedure for unfair prejudice petitions is to be found in the Companies (Unfair Prejudice Applications) Proceedings Rules 2009 (SI 2009/2469). Rule 2(2) provides that, except so far as inconsistent with CA 2006 and the Rules, the CPR apply to s.994 petitions with any necessary modification. It is as a result of this Rule that points of claim and defences fall to be treated as "statements of case" to which the CPR apply: *Re Bankside Hotels Ltd* [2018] EWHC 1035 (Ch) at [138]. But where the defence to a s.994 petition has been struck out, the petitioner still had to satisfy the court with evidence that relief should be granted to him, and CPR 3.5 (allegation not denied is admitted) did not apply: *ibid*. **9-30**

To the end of the paragraph, add:
　Petitions in the High Court are now presented and heard in the Business and Property Courts, and allocated to its Insolvency and Companies List (Chancery Division). The name "Business and Property Courts" is considered a more intel- **9-30**

ligible and user-friendly name in the contemporary world than simply "Chancery Division".

To the end of the paragraph, add:

9-32   The Practice Note dated 22 April 2015 requires the parties to provide before the first directions hearing non-binding estimates of the value of the shares in issue so as to assist the court in meaningful costs management. This does not go as far as the practice first piloted in 2014 by the Supreme Court of Victoria and now Practice Note SC CC 8 (revised 2018) which envisages consideration particularly in the case of smaller businesses, at the earliest stage, of directions for a non-binding independent valuation of the shares and for a mediation, on the underlying assumption that commonly the dispute between the parties is the value of the shares, it being probable that one party will have to buy out the other: see *Yung Yui Kwai v Yung Woon Kwai* [2017] HKEC 2824 at [7]. There is much to be commended in this approach. In the event, the court in *Yung Yui Kwai* accepted that it had jurisdiction to appoint a valuer before trial to value a company with a view to facilitating settlement and the narrowing of issues, but it declined to do so. See also the notes under para.8-168.

Practice Note SC CC 8 (revised 2018) of the Supreme Court of Victoria states:

"*4. BACKGROUND*

4.1   Many applications each month are issued in the Court seeking relief under s 233 of the Act where it is alleged that the affairs of a company have been conducted in an oppressive manner. Under the Rules, such applications must be commenced by originating process. Unless the Court otherwise directs, the originating process must be supported by an affidavit stating the facts in support of the process and must annexe an ASIC search of the company.

4.2   A large percentage of the claims seeking relief under s 233 of the Act relate to small businesses, most commonly family businesses. Frequently, the value of the business is not substantial. Nevertheless, applications are often supported by affidavits which run to many pages and considerable detail. At the first return of the originating process, it is common for orders to be made for inspection and copying of the books of the company, for valuation of the shares in the company and for mediation.

4.3   On 1 October 2014, the Court commenced operating a pilot program in respect of oppression applications (Pilot). The Court embarked on this course with a view to facilitating the just, efficient, timely and cost effective resolution of the real issues in dispute in applications under s 233 of the Act. In particular, the Pilot sought to trial initiatives aimed at exploring resolution of the dispute at a very early stage of the proceeding before significant costs had been incurred.

4.4   The Pilot set out a streamlined procedure for the case management of oppression proceedings in the Court. During the life of the Pilot, a significant number of matters were commenced and subject to the new process. The Pilot resulted in the early resolution of a number of those matters or, where early resolution was not practicable, a significant narrowing of the issues in dispute.

4.5   The Court has now resolved to continue the procedure under the Pilot on an ongoing basis.

5. OPPRESSION PROCEEDING PROGRAM

5.1   From 18 May 2018, and subject to any contrary order of the Court, the following procedure will apply in respect of applications under s 233 of the Act (whether or not other relief is also sought).

5.2   Applications for relief are to be made by originating process filed via RedCrest and supported by an affidavit which:
(a)   is no more than three pages in length;

(b) sets out a clear and succinct summary of the facts alleged to constitute the acts of oppression;
(c) sets out a preliminary estimate of the value of the shares in the company (where practicable);
(d) exhibits a current ASIC search of the company; and
(e) has no other exhibits.

5.3 In preparing the affidavit, practitioners should have regard to the relevant authorities which provide examples of the type of conduct that may ground a claim under s 233 of the Act.

5.4 Upon initiation, the matter will be entered into the Judge-managed Corporations List and will attract an Entry into List fee in accordance with regulation 9 of the *Supreme Court (Fees) Interim Regulations 2017* (Vic).

5.5 The Corporations List Judge will review the proceeding to decide whether it is a matter which lends itself to management under the Program or whether the characteristics of the case suggest it would be more appropriately managed and determined by a Judge. For example, it is unlikely that the procedure will be appropriate if the application concerns a publicly listed company or involves complex trust structures. If the matter is suitable for inclusion in the Program, the Corporations List Judge will formally refer the matter on the papers.

5.6 Following entry into the Program and the filing of a notice of appearance by the Defendant(s), the application will be made returnable for an initial conference before an Associate Judge or a Judicial Registrar. The parties (as well as their practitioners) will be expected to attend that conference. The Associate Judge or Judicial Registrar will explore with the parties whether the matter is ready for referral to mediation or whether any preliminary steps are required to be undertaken, for example, whether:

5.6.1 the Defendant(s) should first be afforded an opportunity to file a responding affidavit of no more than three pages;

5.6.2 a valuation of the company should be arranged; or

5.6.3 an order for access and inspection of the books of the company should be made. Orders for points of claim, points of defence and more detailed affidavits are unlikely to be made until after the mediation.

5.7 A number of matters will be listed for initial conference before an Associate Judge or Judicial Registrar on the same day. Whilst the parties are encouraged to adopt a pragmatic and collaborative approach to identifying any necessary preliminary steps, consent orders will not be made in advance of the initial conference.

5.8 If urgent orders are sought at the initial conference that are beyond the jurisdiction of Associate Judges or the Judicial Registrar, or for some other reason the presiding judicial officer forms the view that the application should be referred back to the Corporations List Judge, then that referral will be made.

5.9 Matters under the Program will generally be mediated by either an Associate Judge or a Judicial Registrar. In some cases, the matter may be considered appropriate for referral to external private mediation.

5.10 If a matter does not resolve at the mediation, an Associate Judge or Judicial Registrar may make consent directions for the future conduct of the matter.

Once these steps have been completed, and if the dispute has not resolved, the application may be referred to a judge for further directions and/or hearing."

The standard form for valuation provides (Sch.2 to Practice Note SC CC1 of the Supreme Court of Victoria):

"THE COURT ORDERS THAT:

1. An independent person ("the Valuer") be appointed to express an opinion as to the value of the shares of # ("the Company").
2. The Valuer be a person agreed upon by the parties by 4.00 pm on # .
3. Pursuant to s 247A of the Corporations Act 2001 (Cth), the plaintiff and one

representative of each of his or her legal and accounting advisers is authorised to inspect the books (as the term "books" is defined in s 9 of the Corporations Act 2001 (Cth)) of the Company.
4. The defendant by its officers and employees, including #, must make the books of the Company available for inspection and copying in accordance with paragraph 3 of these orders between the hours of 9.00 am and 5.00 pm commencing on # and ending on #.
5. The plaintiff provide to the Valuer a copy of each document which the parties or either of them wish the Valuer to see for the purposes of the valuation by 4.00 pm on #.
6. Any submission which either party wishes to make to the Valuer be in writing and provided to the Valuer and to the other party by 4.00 pm on #.
7. The Valuer may inspect all or any of the books of the Company for the purposes of the valuation.
8. Each party must comply with the reasonable requests of the Valuer, including for the provision of any information or documents including copy documents, as soon as reasonably practicable after the making of such a request.
9. The Valuer must complete the valuation and provide a copy to the parties and the Court by 4.00 pm on #.
10. The parties pay the costs of the Valuer in equal shares in the first instance.
11. The further hearing of the summons for directions is adjourned to #.
12. Liberty to apply is reserved to the parties and the Valuer on reasonable notice.
13. Costs are reserved."

Further information and disclosure

To the end of the paragraph, add:

9-37   A without prejudice offer from the respondents to sell the petitioner the company shares for an increased amount, on the basis that they knew of alleged wrongdoing that could lead to the company taking committal proceedings against him, had amounted to blackmail and fell within the unambiguous impropriety exception to privilege, and the petitioner would therefore be permitted to rely on it in his unfair prejudice petition: *Ferster v Ferster* [2016] C.P. Rep. 42.

To the end of the paragraph, add:

9-37   In *Re Edwardian Group Ltd* [2017] EWHC 2805 (Ch) it was held that petitioners were entitled to redact documents about litigation funding so as to remove passages which evidenced the substance of legal advice.

Pro-active case management and the determination of issues at a preliminary stage

Replace paragraph 9-47 with:

9-47   In *Re Annacott Holdings Ltd* [2012] EWCA Civ 998, it was said that generally a split trial of liability and quantum will be ordered: see at [27] of the judgment of Arden LJ. But the overriding objectives of the CPR have the habit of sounding good but being difficult to achieve in practice in complex and weighty litigation, as petitions on the statutory grounds often are. The court is often in the dark as to the real state of the dispute between the parties. The concept of unfair prejudice is diffuse and does not easily lend itself to the identification of key issues. The court cannot be expected to wave its magic wand and give the necessary directions of its own motion: it requires the parties to formulate specific proposals, for example as to the formulation of preliminary issues, for the court's consideration: *Re Rotadata Ltd* [2000] B.C.C. 686 Ch D (Comp). Furthermore, although it is unfashionable to say so in the light of the contrary indications in the *Chancery Guide* (2016), there is much to be said in many cases in this area of the law, in terms of cost-effectiveness, speed, the reasonable expectations of the parties, the prospect of appeals, and pressure to reach a final settlement without a trial, for the "old-fashioned" idea of a single trial of all the live issues, including valuation and/or quantum: *Electrical Waste Recycling v City Electrical Factors* [2012] EWHC 38 (Ch); *Roadchef (Employees Benefits Trustees) Ltd v Ingram Hill* [2013] EWHC 939 (Ch); and see para.9-49 below. The real issue between the parties, although this will usually be hidden from the court behind the veil of "without prejudice" communications, is likely to relate to valuation and the longer the determination of that issue is postponed the longer the dispute, including in particular the dispute over entitlement to costs, will last, to the detriment of the party with the fewer resources.[23] It is very easy for a party resisting a single trial of all the issues to assert that this will save costs, when the opposite is its real motivation. The same sentiments are reflected in the practice of the Supreme Court of Victoria—refer to the notes under para.9-32 above. It may be necessary first to assess the fair value of the shares sought to be purchased in order to decide whether a share purchase order would be a proportionate remedy: see *VB Football Assets v Blackpool Football Club (Properties) Ltd* [2017] EWHC 2767 (Ch) at [426].

[23] It is therefore a useful step in the right direction that the parties are now routinely ordered to exchange non-binding share valuations at an early stage: see para.9-32(3) above.

To the end of the paragraph, add:

See also *McLoughlin v Grovers* [2002] Q.B. 1312 (CA) at [66] on the undesirability of a preliminary issue hearing unless it will be determinative of the outcome of the proceedings.

9-49

CHAPTER 10

Winding-up on the Just and Equitable Ground

TABLE OF CONTENTS

Principle 15—just and equitable	10-01■
Locus Standi	10-09
Tangible Interest	10-16
Relationship with the Unfair Prejudice Remedy	10-22
Grounds for Winding-up on Just and Equitable Basis	10-26■
Discretion	10-57
Procedure	10-58■
Collateral Purpose and Alternative Remedies Generally	10-63
Arbitration Agreements	10-65

PRINCIPLE 15—JUST AND EQUITABLE

To the end of the paragraph, add:

See now CPR PD—Insolvency Proceedings—Part 7 (Unfair Prejudice Petitions, Winding Up and Validation Orders): undesirability of claiming winding up on just and equitable ground in the alternative to relief on the unfair prejudice ground as a matter of course.

10-08

GROUNDS FOR WINDING-UP ON JUST AND EQUITABLE BASIS

Breakdown of trust and confidence

To the end of the paragraph, add:

In *Badyal v Badyal* [2018] EWHC 68 (Ch) it was reaffirmed that a mere breakdown in trust and confidence cannot of itself amount to either unfair prejudice or grounds for winding up on the just and equitable basis: [113]–[119]. But the point does not appear to have been fully argued.

10-53

PROCEDURE

Replace first paragraph with:

The procedure for the presentation and prosecution of a winding-up petition by a shareholder on the just and equitable ground is governed by rr.7.25-7.36 of the Insolvency Rules 2016. In the High Court such a petition is assigned to the Business and Property Courts, Company and Insolvency List (Chancery). The jurisdic-

10-58

tion of county courts is limited by s.117 of the 1986 Act. Only certain county courts even have that limited jurisdiction and the usual practice in anything but the most straightforward case is to present the petition in the High Court. The High Court has unlimited jurisdiction and in London the matter is assigned to the Chancery Division, Companies Court.

To the end of the paragraph, add:

10-61 See now CPR PD—Insolvency Proceedings—Part 7 (Unfair Prejudice Petitions, Winding Up and Validation Orders): undesirability of claiming winding up on just and equitable ground in the alternative to relief on the unfair prejudice ground as a matter of course.

In *Re Fortuna Development Corp* [2004–5] CILR 533, Henderson J held that in the case of a solvent company, the following four elements had to be established before an applicant would be entitled to a validation order:

1. the proposed disposition must appear to be within the powers of the directors;
2. the evidence must show that the directors believe the disposition is necessary or expedient in the interests of the company;
3. it must appear that in reaching the decision to make the disposition the directors have acted in good faith (the burden of establishing bad faith being on the party opposing the application); and
4. the reasons for the disposition must be shown to be ones which an intelligent and honest director could reasonably hold.

See also *Aurora Funds Management Ltd v Torchlight GP Ltd* unreported, 27 April 2018 (CICA).

CHAPTER 11

Personal Rights of Shareholders

TABLE OF CONTENTS

Principle 2—separate legal personality and lifting the veil	11-01
Principle 3—personal rights of individual shareholder	11-02■
The Shareholder's Loss—and Reflective Loss	11-14■
A Cause of Action Vested in the Shareholder	11-23
Claim v An Outsider	11-25■
Claim v Another Insider	11-35■
Piercing the Corporate Veil	11-79■

PRINCIPLE 3—PERSONAL RIGHTS OF INDIVIDUAL SHAREHOLDER

Replace paragraph 11-12 with:

A useful starting point for illustration purposes is the question of an auditor's liability to the shareholders, as opposed to the auditor's professional client, i.e. the company, for negligence in the preparation of audited accounts. Lord Bridge held in *Caparo Industries Plc v Dickman* [1990] 2 A.C. 605 HL at 626:

11-12

> "No doubt these provisions [in the Companies Acts relating to audited accounts] establish a relationship between the auditors and the shareholders of a company on which the shareholder is entitled to rely for the protection of his interest. But the crucial question concerns the extent of the shareholder's interest which the auditor has a duty to protect. The shareholders of a company have a collective interest in the company's proper management and in so far as a negligent failure of the auditor to report accurately on the state of the company's finances deprives the shareholders of the opportunity to exercise their powers in general meeting to call the directors to book and to ensure that errors in management are corrected, the shareholders ought to be entitled to a remedy. But in practice no problem arises in this regard since the interest of the shareholders in the proper management of the company's affairs is indistinguishable from the interest of the company itself and any loss suffered by the shareholders, e.g. by the negligent failure of the auditor to discover and expose a misappropriation of funds by a director of the company, will be recouped by a claim against the auditors in the name of the company, not by individual shareholders."

The starting point for determining whether a parent company owed a duty to those affected by its subsidiary's operations was the three-part test in *Caparo Industries Plc v Dickman* [1990] 2 A.C. 605 (HL): *Lungowe v Vedanta Resources Plc* [2017] B.C.C. 787.

THE SHAREHOLDER'S LOSS—AND REFLECTIVE LOSS

Replace paragraph 11-18 with:

11-18 A summary of the relevant principles[6] (the italicised passages are the qualifications deriving from the judgment of Chadwick LJ in *Giles v Rhind* [2003] 2 W.L.R. 237 at [61]–[62]: see *Webster v Sandersons* [2009] 2 B.C.L.C. 542 at [36]–[37]) is set out in [33] of the judgment of Neuberger LJ in *Gardner v Parker* [2005] B.C.C. 46:

> "(1) a loss claimed by a shareholder which is merely reflective of a loss suffered by the company—i.e. a loss which would be made good if the company had enforced in full its rights against the defendant wrongdoer—is not recoverable by the shareholder *save in a case where by reason of the wrong done to it, the company is unable to pursue its claim against the wrongdoer*;
>
> (2) where there is no reasonable doubt that that is the case, the court can properly act, in advance of trial, to strike out the offending heads of claim;
>
> (3) The irrecoverable loss (being merely reflective of the company's loss) is not confined to the individual claimant's loss of dividends on his shares or diminution in the value of his shareholding in the company but extends ... to 'all other payments which the shareholder might have obtained from the company if it had not been deprived of its funds' and also to other payments which the company would have made if it had had the necessary funds even if the plaintiff would have received them qua employee and not qua shareholder *save that this does not apply to the loss of future benefits to which the claimant had an expectation but no contractual entitlement*;
>
> (4) the principle is not rooted simply in the avoidance of double recovery in fact; it extends to heads of loss which the company could have claimed but has chosen not to and therefore includes the case where the company has settled for less than it might ...;
>
> (5) provided the loss claimed by the shareholder is merely reflective of the company's loss and provided the defendant wrongdoer owed duties both to the company and to the shareholder, it is irrelevant that the duties so owed may be different in content."[7]

The rule against the recovery of reflective loss applies as much to creditors of the company in question as it does to shareholders: *Garcia v Marex Financial Ltd* [2018] EWCA Civ 1468, approving *Peak Hotels and Resorts Ltd v Tarek Investments Ltd* [2015] EWHC 3048 (Ch), and *St Vincent European General Partner Ltd v Robinson* [2018] EWHC 1230 (Comm). Contrast *Latin American Investments Ltd v Maroil Trading Inc* [2017] EWHC 1254 (Comm) where it was held that it was arguable that the availability of an order for specific performance to enforce the terms of a shareholders' agreement gave the claimant a personal claim which did not fall foul of the rule against reflective loss.

---

[6] The principles have been applied in a number of cases: *Humberclyde Finance Group Ltd v Hicks* unreported 4 November 2001 Ch D (Neuberger J); *Day v Cook* [2003] 1 B.C.C. 256; *Shaker v Al-Bedrawi* [2003] Ch. 350; *Ellis v Property Leeds (UK) Ltd* [2002] 2 B.C.L.C. 175; *Gardner v Parker* [2005] B.C.C. 46; *Giles v Rhind* [2003] Ch. 618; *Perry v Day* [2005] 2 B.C.L.C. 405; *Malhotra v Malhotra* [2015] 1 B.C.L.C. 428 at [53]–[63]; *Barclay Pharmaceuticals Ltd v Waypharm LP* [2013] 2 B.C.L.C. 551; *International Leisure Ltd v First National Trustee Co UK Ltd* [2013] Ch. 346; *Sivagnanam v Barclays Bank Plc* [2015] EWHC 3985 (Comm). In *Waddington Ltd v Chan Chun Hoo Thomas* [2009] 2 B.C.L.C. 82, Lord Millett, sitting as a judge of the Hong Kong Final Court of Appeal, stated that *Giles v Rhind* was wrongly decided, but it is binding in the UK: *Webster v Sandersons* [2009] 2 B.C.L.C. 542 at [36]–[37].

[7] Applied in *Webster v Sandersons* [2009] 2 B.C.L.C. 542, and *Sukhoruchkin v Van Bekestein* [2013] EWHC 1993 (Ch).

Replace paragraph 11-20 with:

11-20 In *Giles v Rhind*,[9] the Court of Appeal held that there was[10] an exception to the fundamental principle established in the *Gore Wood (1)* case that a shareholder could not recover loss which was merely reflective of the loss suffered by the company, such as the diminution in value of his shares. The exception in question arose where it was the defendant's wrongdoing which prevented the company from enforcing its claim. The facts were that the defendant (a major shareholder) had entered into a shareholders' and subscription agreement with the company, the claimant (another major shareholder), and an outside investor. The defendant, after leaving the company, in effect stole the company's business. The claimant established at trial that the defendant, in so doing, had broken covenants given in the shareholders' agreement for the protection of his investment. An issue arose in the damages inquiry as to the claimant's ability to recover loss which was reflective of the loss suffered by the company. The company had been forced into administration and had discontinued its action against the defendant due to shortage of funds. Chadwick LJ held at [64]–[67], that the *Gore Wood (1)* case was distinguishable on the issue of causation:

"[66] To put the point more starkly, the effect of the judge's decision—as he himself recognised—is that a wrongdoer who, in breach of his contract with the company and its shareholders, 'steals' the whole of the company's business, with the intention that the company should be so denuded of funds that it cannot pursue its remedy against him, and who gives effect to that intention by an application for security for costs which his own breach of contract has made it impossible for the company to provide, is entitled to defeat a claim by the shareholders on the grounds that their claim is 'trumped' by the claim which his own conduct was calculated to prevent, and has in fact prevented, the company from pursuing. If that were, indeed, the law following the decision in *Johnson v Gore Wood & Co* [2002] 2 A.C. 1, I would not find it easy to reconcile the result with Lord Bingham of Cornhill's observation, at p 36c, that 'the court must be astute to ensure that the party who has in fact suffered loss is not arbitrarily denied fair compensation'.

[67] In my view the reasoning in *Johnson v Gore Wood & Co* does not compel the conclusion that the law requires that result … ."

Recent cases show how narrow is the so-called "exception", established by *Giles v Rhind*, to the rule against the recovery of reflective loss. The exception only applies where the defendant's wrongdoing has made it *legally impossible* for the company to sue: it is not enough that the defendant has denuded the company of funds so as to make it factually impossible because of its impecuniosity for it to sue: *Garcia v Marex Financial Ltd* [2018] EWCA Civ 1468, approving *Peak Hotels and Resorts Ltd v Tarek Investments Ltd* [2015] EWHC 3048 (Ch), and *St Vincent European General Partner Ltd v Robinson* [2018] EWHC 1230 (Comm).

[9] Judgment in the subsequent hearing of the assessment of damages in the *Giles v Rhind* case was in [2004] 1 B.C.L.C. 385.

[10] Waller LJ appears to have only held that it was arguable.

CLAIM V AN OUTSIDER

To the end of the paragraph, add:

A bank which gave a credit reference to a credit reference agency owed no duty of care to that agent's undisclosed principal: *Playboy Club London Ltd v Banca Nazionale del Lavoro SpA* [2018] UKSC 43.

11-27

CLAIM V ANOTHER INSIDER

Fiduciary Duty owed by directors to shareholders

To the end of the paragraph, add:

11-46   *Sharp v Blank* [2015] EWHC 3220 (Ch) is now reported at [2017] B.C.C. 187. Newey J provided the following summary of the law whether directors owed their duties to the company alone:

> "[9] The general principles are well established:
>
> (1) The directors of a company owe fiduciary duties to the company. This is unexceptionable and flows from the fact that the directors are agents of the company and stewards of its affairs. As Mummery LJ puts it in *Peskin v Anderson* [2001] B.C.C. 874 at [33] the fiduciary duties owed by directors to the company "arise from the relationship between the directors and the company directed and controlled by them"; it is the fact that they are directors of the company's affairs which by itself gives rise to their fiduciary duties.
>
> (2) But in general the directors do not, solely by virtue of their office of director, owe fiduciary duties to the shareholders, collectively or individually: *Peskin v Anderson* (above) at [29]. As pointed out by Handley JA in the New South Wales Court of Appeal in *Brunninghausen v Glavanics* [1999] NSWCA 199; (1999) 32 A.C.S.R. 294 at [40], this is in essence no more than an application of the principle established by *Salomon v A Salomon & Co Ltd* [1897] A.C. 22 that a company is distinct from its members. The directors direct and control the affairs and assets of the company; they do not direct or control the affairs or assets of the members.
>
> (3) The general principle that directors do not owe fiduciary duties to shareholders has also been said to be supported by a number of policy considerations. Handley JA in *Brunninghausen* (above) referred to the fact that only the company, not its members, can sue for wrongs done to the company (under the rule in *Foss v Harbottle* (1843) 2 Hare 461), and the principle that where a wrong has been done to a company, individual shareholders are not able to sue for losses which are merely derivative or reflective (as exemplified by *Prudential Assurance Co Ltd v Newman Industries Ltd (No.2)* [1982] Ch. 204 and *Stein v Blake* [1998] B.C.C. 316—this is of course not a complete explanation as some losses claimed by shareholders go beyond merely reflective loss (as indeed in the present case). Handley JA also said that if the directors owed fiduciary duties to the shareholders they would be liable to harassing actions by minority shareholders, and exposed to a multiplicity of actions, each shareholder having his own personal claim. This latter point was also made by Mummery LJ in *Peskin v Anderson* (above) at [30] where he said that it was important that directors are not overexposed to the risk of multiple legal actions by dissenting minority shareholders. At first instance in the same case Neuberger J said that to hold that a director owed some sort of general fiduciary duty to shareholders would involve placing an unfair, unrealistic and uncertain burden on a director, and would present him frequently with a position where his duty to shareholders would be in conflict with his undoubted duty to the company: [2000] B.C.C. 1110 at 1121. The idea of a potential conflict between the directors' duty to the company and their supposed duty to shareholders can also be found in *Percival v Wright* [1902] 2 Ch. 421, often regarded as the origin of this line of authority, where Swinfen Eady J referred to the fact that if directors owed a duty to disclose negotiations to shareholders it would place them in a most invidious position, as premature disclosure of negotiations might well be against the best interests of the company.
>
> (4) The actual decision in *Percival v Wright* (above) has had a chequered history which it is not necessary to recount; whatever the merits of the actual decision,

the general principle that directors do not owe fiduciary duties to their shareholders is confirmed by *Peskin v Anderson* and is not in doubt.

[10] There are however circumstances where directors have been held to owe particular fiduciary duties to shareholders. The duties that arise in such cases are dependent on establishing a 'special factual relationship' between the directors and the shareholders in the particular case: *Peskin v Anderson* (above) per Mummery LJ at [33]. ..."

The learned judge proceeded to analyse a number of cases where such a special relationship had been established or canvassed in the judgment, which he observed were all concerned with closely-held companies. After referring again to *Peskin v Anderson*, he continued:

"[12] I take it therefore to be established law, binding on me, that although a director of a company can owe fiduciary duties to the company's shareholders, he does not do so by the mere fact of being a director, but only where there is on the facts of the particular case a "special relationship" between the director and the shareholders. It seems to me to follow that this special relationship must be something over and above the usual relationship that any director of a company has with its shareholders. It is not enough that the director, as a director, has more knowledge of the company's affairs than the shareholders have: since they direct and control the company's affairs this will almost inevitably be the case. Nor is it enough that the actions of the directors will have the potential to affect the shareholders—again this will always, or almost always, be the case. On the decided cases the sort of relationship that has given rise to a fiduciary duty has been where there has been some personal relationship or particular dealing or transaction between them.

[13] I do not find this surprising. A fiduciary, as explained by Millett LJ in his classic judgment in *Bristol & West Building Society v Mothew* [1998] Ch. 1 at 18A–F, is someone who has undertaken to act for or on behalf of another in circumstances which give rise to a relationship of trust and confidence. That is why the distinguishing obligation of a fiduciary is the obligation of loyalty: someone who has agreed to act in the interests of another has to put the interests of that other first. But the relationship between directors and shareholders is not in general like that. A director is a fiduciary for his company: by agreeing to act as director, he necessarily agrees to act in the interests of the company. But he does not have, by virtue of his appointment as director, any direct relationship with the shareholders: no doubt the interests of the shareholders and the company are in general aligned but this does not mean that a director has agreed to act for the individual shareholders or has a direct relationship with them—his relationship is with the company. If he is to be held to owe fiduciary duties to the individual shareholders, there must be something unusual in the nature of the relationship which gives rise to it. That no doubt explains why the cases where such a duty has been held to exist mostly concern companies which are small and closely held, where there is often a family or other personal relationship between the parties, and where, in almost all cases, there is a particular transaction involved in which directors are dealing with the shareholders, from which the directors often stand to benefit personally. The imposition of a fiduciary duty in such circumstances reflects the fact that directors who have a close family or other personal relationship with shareholders, and are entering into transactions with them, may be tempted to exploit that relationship to take unfair advantage of the shareholders for their own benefit."

To the end of the paragraph, add:
See also *Dusik v Newton* (1985) 62 B.C.L.R. 1, *Crawley v Short* [2009] NSWCA 410, and *Valastiak v Valastiak* [2010] BCCA 71, cited by Newey J in *Sharp v Blank* [2017] B.C.C. 187 at [10(5)]. For *Crawley v Short*, see the notes under para.7-106.

11-55

Joint ventures—equitable constraints in relationships between shareholders

To the end of the paragraph, add:

11-58 The recent decision of the Court of Appeal in *Generator Developments Ltd v Lidl UK GmbH* [2018] EWCA Civ 396 further demonstrates the need for clarification at the highest level of this whole field, namely the basis upon and circumstances in which equity will intervene in what may be loosely described as joint ventures, on one or more of the traditional equitable principles of estoppel, common intention constructive trust and the existence of a fiduciary relationship. This field is relevant to the unfair prejudice remedy, and in particular to the basis upon and circumstances in which the conduct of the majority is deemed to be "unfair", in the light of Lord Hoffmann's seminal speech in *O'Neill v Phillips* that unfairness must be determined by "tolerably well settled" or "traditional" "equitable principles" as opposed to some broader notions of fairness: see para.7-18, and the tension that this dictum creates as shown in the debate at paras 7-36–7-38, and the discussion about understandings binding in honour alone as opposed to contract ("a gentleman's agreement") at paras 7-85, 7-102, 7-111–7-115, and at 11-67 (where *O'Neill v Phillips* is contrasted with the *Banner Homes* line of authority). In the *Lidl* case, Lewison LJ, criticising aspects of the judgment of Chadwick LJ in the *Banner Homes* case, held that the critical factor in the earlier decision of Goulding J in *Island Holdings Ltd v Birchington Engineering Co Ltd* unreported, 7 July 1981 was the finding of a fiduciary relationship between the joint venturers despite the co-existence of "subject to contract" discussions: at [42]. He agreed with Etherton LJ in *Crossco No.4 Unltd v Jolan Ltd* [2011] EWCA Civ 1619 that the basis of the *Pallant v Morgan* [1953] Ch. 43 equity was the existence of a fiduciary relationship: [71]. But he felt bound to follow the majority view in the *Crossco v Jolan* case that this equity was the imposition of a constructive trust: [72]. In holding that on the facts it was clear that equity would not intervene. Lewison LJ said at [79]:

> "Second, the proposed 'joint venture' (if such it was) was expressly made 'subject to contract'... That phrase appeared (three times) in all three versions of the heads of terms that passed back and forth between the parties well before contracts were exchanged for the land purchase. The meaning of that phrase is well-known. What it means is that (a) neither party intends to be bound either in law or in equity unless and until a formal contract is made; and (b) that each party reserves the right to withdraw until such time as a binding contract is made. It follows, therefore, that in negotiating on that basis both Generator and Lidl took the commercial risk that one or other of them might back out of the proposed transaction. As Lord Walker stressed in Cobbe, equity will not intervene in a case where the parties expressly agree that a putative agreement is binding in honour only. Likewise, in the Hong Kong case [[1987] A.C. 114] the Privy Council recognised that the use of the 'subject to contract' formula means that the parties are not committed either in law or in equity. Like Mr Cobbe, Generator never expected to acquire any interest in the land otherwise than by way of a legally enforceable contract. To put the point another way, where negotiations in a commercial context are expressly made 'subject to contract' there is no understanding or arrangement capable of bringing the first of Chadwick LJ's requirements into play. The mere fact that parties have agreed to engage in good faith negotiations for the making of a joint venture agreement is insufficient to support a constructive trust: Kilcarne Holdings Ltd v Targetfollow (Birmingham) Ltd [2005] EWCA Civ 1355 at [15] and [23]. In short, a 'subject to contract' agreement is no agreement at all. For the same reason, the consequence of an express non-agreement is that fiduciary duties will not arise. Mr Gaunt argued that there was a difference between an understanding in principle that there would be 'a' joint venture, which was not 'subject to contract', and the detailed terms of such a venture which were. He also argued that although the 'subject to contract' reservation applied to the terms of the proposed joint

venture agreement, it did not apply to the acquisition of the land. I do not consider that that is a sound distinction. It would subvert the well-understood meaning and effect of negotiations 'subject to contract" to differentiate the acquisition of the land, the principle of a joint venture and the 'terms of the putative joint venture agreement in that way. Moreover, it appears that Mr Barnes purported to draw that very distinction in paragraph 67 of his witness statement; but, as the judge recorded at [45], when asked about it in cross-examination he accepted that he struggled 'to get to the finer points of what's meant there'. That goes to show that the proposed distinction is an artificial one, which would not have been in the minds of the parties at the time. Moreover, it was always intended, right from the inception of discussions, that the parties' respective rights and obligations would be regulated by written contracts." (Emphasis added.)

See also *John Alexander's Clubs Pty Ltd v White City Tennis Club Ltd* [2010] 241 C.L.R. 1 (HCA), in which it was held that no fiduciary relationship should be superimposed upon a contractual one and a *Pallant v Morgan* constructive trust was not imposed; the interests of a third party, such as a mortgagee, should be considered.

For other recent cases in this field, see *Baturina v Chistyakov* [2017] EWHC 1049 (Comm); *Farrar v Miller* [2018] EWCA Civ 172.

For the enforcement of "a gentleman's agreement" in the context of the unfair prejudice remedy, see paras 7-89–7-115, and recent cases such as *VB Football Assets v Blackpool Football Club (Properties) Ltd* [2017] EWHC 2767 (Ch) noted under para.7-94 above. Contrast *Re Edwardian Group Ltd* [2018] EWHC 1715 (Ch), at [213].

In the context of the unfair prejudice remedy, equitable principles of good faith derived from the law of partnership are in appropriate circumstances, i.e. the so-called "quasi-partnership", imported by that remedy: see Ch.7, paras 7-89 et seq.

Fiduciary relationships

To the end of the paragraph, add:
See Principle 16 (equitable principles) discussed at para.3-04 et seq and Principle 9 (shareholder's voting rights as property) discussed at para.5-31 et seq. **11-69**

After "relationship between shareholders.", add:
See also *John Alexander's Clubs Pty Ltd v White City Tennis Club Ltd* [2010] 241 C.L.R. 1 (HCA). **11-76**

PIERCING THE CORPORATE VEIL

To the end of the paragraph, add:
Petrodel Resources Ltd v Prest [2013] 2 A.C. 415 was applied by the Privy Council in *Persad v Singh* [2017] B.C.C. 779—the court held that the corporate veil could not be pierced. **11-80**

Equating the company with its shareholders

To the end of the paragraph, add:
See *Singularis Holdings Ltd (In Liquidation) v Daiwa Capital Markets Europe Ltd* [2018] 1 W.L.R. 2777. **11-85**

To the end of the paragraph, add:
For a case where the director responsible for unsuccessful litigation by a **11-86**

company was not held liable for the costs, see *JAS Financial Products LLP v ICAP Plc* [2017] EWHC 1172 (Comm)

CHAPTER 12

Foreign Element

TABLE OF CONTENTS

Section 994 of the Companies Act	12-01
Winding-up on the Just and Equitable Ground	12-04
Derivative Claims	12-08
Other Shareholder Disputes	12-10
Conflict of Laws	12-14
The European Dimension	12-18■

THE EUROPEAN DIMENSION

Replace paragraph 12-27 with:

12-27 Where the claimant has founded jurisdiction on art.2 of the Brussels Convention on the basis of the defendants' domicile in a Contracting State, that state cannot decline jurisdiction on forum conveniens grounds in favour of the courts of a non-contracting state: see *Owusu v Jackson*.[17] *Owusu v Jackson* was explained in *Lungowe v Vedanta Resources Plc* [2017] B.C.C. 787. It was held that the position was clear: art.4 of the Recast Brussels Regulation, in materially identical terms to the Brussels Convention 1968 art.2, precluded the English court from declining jurisdiction where the defendant was a company domiciled in England and Wales.

---

[17] The flaws in this decision of the European Court are well stated in A. Briggs, "The death of Harrods: forum non conveniens and the European Court" (2005) 121 L.Q.R. 535. See *Choudhary v Bhattar* [2010] 2 B.C.L.C. 17 at [48]–[54].

CHAPTER 14

Limited and Limited Liability Partnerships

TABLE OF CONTENTS

The Statutory Remedies for the Protection of Minorities .. 14-13
Derivative Claims and the Rule in Foss v Harbottle ...... 14-17■

DERIVATIVE CLAIMS AND THE RULE IN FOSS V HARBOTTLE

LLPs

To the end of the paragraph, add:
See *Harris v Microfusion 2003-2 LLP* [2017] 1 B.C.L.C. 305, noted under para.6-20, where it was common ground that the rule in *Foss v Harbottle* did apply to derivative claims brought at common law for the benefit of LLPs.   **14-18**

INDEX

This index has been prepared using Sweet and Maxwell's Legal Taxonomy. Main index entries conform to keywords provided by the Legal Taxonomy except where references to specific documents or non-standard terms (denoted by quotation marks) have been included. These keywords provide a means of identifying similar concepts in other Sweet & Maxwell publications and on-line services to which keywords from the Legal Taxonomy have been applied. Readers may find some minor differences between terms used in the text and those which appear in the index. Suggestions to *sweetandmaxwell.taxonomy@tr.com*.

Articles of association
see also Special resolutions
alteration
   court intervention, 5-50
   special resolutions, 3-62, 5-46
exit routes, 7-194
interpretation
   generally, 3-18
   ordinary principles of contract law, 3-19
Breach of contract
unfair prejudice
   incomplete agreements, 7-85
Conflict of interest
directors' duties
   strictness of no conflict rule, 4-68, 4-71
   terminated directorships, 4-93
   weakened directorships, 4-93
no conflict rule
   alteration by articles of association, 4-83
   strictness of no conflict rule, 4-68, 4-71
Conflict of laws
EU law, 12-27
forum conveniens, 12-27
Corporate personality
piercing corporate veil, 11-80, 11-85, 11-86
Costs
orders against shareholders where company is a party, 11-86
share valuation, 8-168
unfair prejudice claims
   generally, 8-168
   offer to buy out petitioner's shares, 8-91
Creditors
directors duties to statutory code, 4-20
Delay
unfair prejudice, 7-205
Derivative claims
alternative remedies, 6-60—6-61
breach of duty by directors, 6-23, 6-26
breach of duty by non-directors, 6-26
bringing a claim, 6-78
causes of action, 6-23, 6-26
Companies Act 2006, 6-08
courts
   discretion of the courts, 6-51, 6-60, 6-61
   permission hearings, 6-43
   threshold criteria, 6-48
criteria

   threshold criteria, 6-48
discretion of courts
   alternative remedies, 6-60—6-61
   double derivative claims, 6-74
   promoting success of company, 6-48
double-derivative claims, 6-74
Foss v Harbottle rule, 6-14, 6-20, 6-22
permission of court
   alternative remedies, 6-60—6-61
   discretion, 6-51, 6-60, 6-61
   inter parte permission hearings, 6-43
   promoting success of company, 6-48
   threshold criteria, 6-48
relationship with unfair prejudice remedy, 7-129
threshold criteria
   duty to promote success of company, 6-48
wrongdoer control, 6-36
Directors
see also Directors' powers and duties
access to company records, 5-23
division of roles with shareholders (Principle 7)
   right to inspect company books and records, 5-23
statutory code
   duty to creditors, 4-20
Directors' powers and duties
breach of duty
   relief by the court, 4-130
Companies Act 2006
   statutory code, 4-20
company records
   access to, 5-23
conflict of interest
   pre-Companies Act, 4-68, 4-71
   strictness and inflexibility of, 4-68, 4-71
   weakened or terminated directorships, 4-93
duties to creditors, 4-20
duties to shareholders
   good faith, 3-26
fiduciary duty
   nature of, 4-31
leaving directors, 4-93
limitation periods, 4-133
modification by shareholders, 4-83
promoting success of company, 6-48
relief from liability

powers of the court, 4-130
success
  duty to promote, 6-48
Discretion
  derivatives claims
    double derivative claim, 6-74
  unfair prejudice, 8-18, 8-28, 8-29
Entrenched provisions
  shareholders' rights
    alteration of Articles, 3-62
Equitable principles
  personal rights of individual shareholders
    generally, 11-58
  Principle 16, 2-21
Fiduciary duty
  directors' duties
    nature of, 4-31
  shareholders' duties, 5-31, 11-46, 11-55
Foreign companies
  EU law, 12-27
Foss v Harbottle rule
  derivative claims
    facts of case, 6-14, 6-20, 6-22
    limited liability partnerships, 14-18
    fraud on the minority, 6-14, 6-20, 6-22
    limited liability partnerships, 14-18
Fraud
  on the minority, 6-14, 6-20, 6-22
Good faith
  duty owed between shareholders
    express contractual duty, 3-26
    majority rule, 5-31
    mutual trust and confidence, 7-117
  express contractual duty, 3-26
Implied terms
  bargain between shareholders
    articles of association, 3-18
    contract law, 3-19
Insolvency
  appointment of receivers, 8-123
  unfair prejudice
    remedies, 8-30
  winding-up, 10-08, 10-58, 10-61
Interim injunctions
  unfair prejudice
    appointment of receivers, 8-123
    freezing orders, 8-126
    generally, 8-114
Interim relief
  see Remedies
Interpretation
  bargain between shareholders
    articles of association, 3-18
    contract law, 3-19
    good faith, 3-26
Joint ventures
  personal rights of shareholders, 11-58
Jurisdiction
  see also Conflict of laws
  EU law, 12-27
  unfair prejudice, 8-01, 8-04

Limited liability partnerships
  derivative claims, 14-18
  Foss v Harbottle rule, 14-18
Liquidators
  provisional liquidators
    appointment, 8-123
  unfair prejudice petitions, 8-30
  winding-up petitions, 10-08, 10-58, 10-61
Locus standi
  unfair prejudice claims, 9-08, 9-17
Majority rule
  see also Derivative claims; Good faith
  basic principles
    voting rights as property (Principle 9), 5-31
  equitable constraints
    expropriation, 5-50
    fiduciary principles, 5-31
    partnerships, 5-46, 5-50
    special resolutions to alter Articles, 5-46
  order in favour of unfair prejudice, 8-01, 8-04
  shares as property (Principle 9), 5-31
  voting rights
    as property, 5-31
Minority shareholders
  basic principles
    equitable principles (Principle 16), 2-21
  discount for share valuation, 8-91
Misconduct
  exclusion cases, 7-142
  good faith
    breach of duty, 7-108
  relationship with the derivative claim, 7-129
Mutual trust and confidence
  good faith
    duty owed between shareholders, 7-117
  partnerships, 7-117
  unfairly prejudicial conduct, 7-117
  winding up, 10-53
Partnerships
  breach of agreements or understandings
    good faith, 7-104, 7-106, 7-108
    incomplete agreements, 7-85
    quasi-partnerships, 7-92, 7-94, 7-96, 7-99, 7-100
    specific expectations and understandings, 7-113
  equitable constraints on majority rule, 5-46, 5-50
  mutual trust and confidence, 7-117
  quasi-partnerships
    generally, 7-92, 7-94, 7-96, 7-99, 7-100
    good faith, 7-104, 7-106, 7-108
    specific expectations and understandings, 7-113
Personal rights
  basic principles
    Principle 3, 11-12
  corporate personality, 11-85, 11-86
  fiduciary duty
    constructive trusts, 11-69
    directors', 11-46, 11-55
    good faith, 11-76
    joint ventures, 11-58

INDEX

shareholders, 11-46, 11-55
piercing corporate veil, 11-80, 11-85, 11-86
shareholders' loss, 11-18, 11-20
third party costs order, 11-86
Piercing the corporate veil
see Corporate personality
Practice and procedure
see Procedure
Principles
principle 3 personal rights of individual shareholder, 11-12
principle 9 voting rights as property, 5-31
principle 15 winding-up on just and equitable basis, 10-08
principle 16 equitable principles, 2-21
Procedure
derivative claims
background, 6-78
unfair prejudice petitions
case management, 9-47, 9-49
disclosure, 9-37
generally, 9-30, 9-32
locus standi, 9-08, 9-17
winding-up petitions, 10-58, 10-61
Provisional liquidators
see Insolvency; Liquidators
"Quasi-partnerships"
existence, 7-92, 7-94, 7-96, 7-99, 7-100
extent of agreements and understandings, 7-113
good faith, 7-104, 7-106, 7-108
Receivers
see Insolvency; Liquidators
Reflective losses
personal rights of shareholders, 11-18, 11-20
Remedies
see also Unfairly prejudicial conduct
shareholder remedies
share purchase orders, 8-48
unfair prejudice
final remedies, 8-01, 8-04
interim remedies, 8-01, 8-04
winding-up
grounds, 7-136
Remuneration
excessive, 7-153, 7-154, 7-165
Separate legal personality
see Corporate personality
Share issues
limitations and laches, 4-133
relief by the court, 4-130
Share valuation
discount for minority status, 8-91
machinery, 8-168
offer to buy out petitioners shares
costs of proceedings, 8-97
out-of-court valuations, 8-172, 8-178, 8-182
valuation basis
allowances for discrete assets or liabilities, 8-159
basis, 8-134, 8-136
date, 8-163, 8-164, 8-165, 8-168
discount for minority shareholding, 8-158

generally, 8-128, 8-131
machinery of, 8-168
out of court, 8-172, 8-178, 8-182
Shareholders
see also Articles of association; Personal rights
access to company records, 5-23
losses of, 11-18, 11-20
no conflict rule
modification, 4-83
principles, 11-12
personal claims (Principle 3)
equity, 11-12
Shareholders' agreements
good faith, 3-26
interpretation
generally, 3-18
ordinary principles of contract law, 3-19
"Shareholders' control"
division of roles with shareholders (Principle 7)
right to inspect company books and records, 5-23
Shares
offers to buy out petitioner's shares
costs of proceedings, 8-97
valuation basis, 8-91
property, as, 5-31
share issues
limitations and laches, 4-133
relief by the court, 4-130
"Share purchase orders"
unfair prejudice
generally, 8-48
Special resolutions
alteration of articles of association
bona fide benefit test, 5-46
court intervention, 5-50
entrenched provisions, 3-62
Third party costs orders
personal rights of shareholders, 11-86
Unfairly prejudicial conduct
see also Good faith
acquiescence, 7-205
application of test
excessive remuneration, 7-153, 7-154, 7-165
exclusion from management, 7-138, 7-142, 7-146
loss of confidence in management, 7-169
procedural irregularities, 7-127
arbitration clauses, 7-198
breach of contract, 7-85
breach of fiduciary duty, 7-127
case law, 7-32, 7-36, 7-37, 7-40
clean hands of petitioner, 7-200, 7-202, 7-204
commercial mismanagement, 7-169
concept, 7-32, 7-36, 7-37, 7-40
conduct of company affairs
acts or omissions, 7-52
costs
generally, 8-97
delay, 7-205

derivative claims
  relationship with unfair prejudice remedy, 7-129
determination of issues, 9-47, 9-49
elements
  conduct of company affairs, 7-52
  interests as shareholders, 7-66, 7-67
  prejudice, 7-74, 7-75
equitable principles
  clean hands, 7-200, 7-202, 7-204
  constructive trusts, 11-69
  Principle 16, 2-21
excessive remuneration, 7-153, 7-154, 7-165
exclusion from management
  employment tribunal proceedings, 7-146
  generally, 7-138, 7-142
exit routes, 7-194
grounds
  breach of agreement or understanding, 7-85, 7-94, 7-96, 7-99, 7-100, 7-104, 7-106, 7-108, 7-113
  breach of directors' duties, 7-127
  mutual trust and confidence, 7-117
  winding-up, 7-136
interests as shareholder, 7-66, 7-67
interim injunctive relief
  appointment of receivers, 8-123
  freezing orders, 8-126
  generally, 8-114
jurisdiction, 8-01, 8-04
locus standi
  entitlement to be registered, 9-08, 9-17
  practice and procedure, 9-08, 9-17
mutual trust and confidence, 7-117
offer to buy
  costs of proceedings, 8-97
  valuation basis, 8-91
out of court valuations, 8-172, 8-178, 8-182
personal rights of individual shareholders
  generally, 11-58
prejudice, 7-74, 7-75
procedural irregularity, 7-127
procedure
  case management, 9-47, 9-49
  disclosure, 9-37
  generally, 9-30, 9-32
  locus standi, 9-08, 9-17
quasi-partnerships
  generally, 7-92, 7-94, 7-96, 7-99, 7-100
  good faith, 7-104, 7-106, 7-108
  specific expectations and understandings, 7-113
relationship with
  derivative claims, 7-129
  winding-up, 7-136, 10-08
remedies
  court's powers, 8-14
  discretion of the court, 8-18, 8-28, 8-29
  final remedies, 8-01, 8-04
  interim injunctive relief, 8-114, 8-123, 8-126
  interim remedies, 8-01, 8-04
  material time, 8-30
  offers to buy out petitioner, 8-91, 8-97
  orders in favour of majority, 8-32
  persons against whom orders made, 8-34, 8-35, 8-37
  provisional liquidators, 8-123
  receivers, 8-123
  share purchase orders, 8-48
share transfers
  death of shareholders, 7-100
share valuation
  allowances for discrete assets or liabilities, 8-159
  basis, 8-134, 8-136
  date, 8-163, 8-164, 8-165, 8-168
  discount for minority shareholding, 8-158
  generally, 8-128, 8-131
  machinery of, 8-168
  out of court, 8-172, 8-178, 8-182
  unfairness, 7-32, 7-36, 7-37, 7-40
  valuation basis, 8-91
winding-up
  grounds, 7-136
  relationship with unfair prejudice remedy, 7-136, 10-08

Validation orders
  objections to, 10-61
Valuation of shares
  see Share valuation
Winding-up
  basic principles, 10-08
  governing rules, 10-58
  grounds for petition
    mutual trust and confidence, 10-53
  interim relief
    interim injunctive relief, 8-114, 8-123, 8-126
    provisional liquidators, 8-123
    receivers, 8-123
  mutual trust and confidence, 10-53
  objections to validation order, 10-61
  procedure, 10-58, 10-61
  provisional liquidators, 8-123
  standard form orders, 10-61
  tangible interest
    general rule, 10-08
  unfair prejudice petitions, 10-58, 10-61
  unfair prejudice remedy (Principle 14)
    grounds for petition, 10-08
    relationship with, 10-08
  validation orders
    objections to, 10-61